TWAYNE'S WORLD AUTHORS SERIES
A Survey of the World's Literature

NEW ZEALAND

Joseph Jones, University of Texas

EDITOR

New Zealand Drama

TWAS 626

NEW ZEALAND DRAMA

By HOWARD McNAUGHTON
University of Canterbury

TWAYNE PUBLISHERS
A DIVISION OF G.K. HALL & CO., BOSTON

Published in 1981 by Twayne Publishers,
A Division of G.K. Hall & Co.
All Rights Reserved

Printed on permanent/durable acid-free paper and bound
in the United States of America

First Printing

Library of Congress Cataloging in Publication Data

McNaughton, Howard Douglas.
New Zealand drama.

(Twayne's world authors series ; TWAS 626 : New Zealand)
Bibliography: p. 157–62
Includes index.
1. New Zealand drama—History and criticism.
I. Title.
PR9631.2.M27   822'.009'9931   80-27870
ISBN 0-8057-6468-2

Contents

About the Author

Howard McNaughton is Senior Lecturer in English at the University of Canterbury and since 1968 has been theater critic for the daily newspaper, *The Press,* Christchurch. He was born in Dunedin in 1945, and is a fifth-generation New Zealander, descended from a precolonial whaler. In 1966, he took an honors degree in Classics at the University of Otago, and subsequently received a M.A. and Ph.D. in English from the University of Canterbury. McNaughton's books include *Contemporary New Zealand Plays* (1974), *New Zealand Drama: A Bibliographical Guide* (1974), and *Bruce Mason* (1976). He has published numerous articles on New Zealand drama and theater history, as well as on Enid Bagnold, Ben Hecht, Jerzy Grotowski, Jane Mander, and Emlyn Williams.

Preface

New Zealand dramatic literature, like the New Zealand theater, has little sense of its own history; playwrights and directors are continually diversifying their work to an extent that would probably not occur if there were a local classic tradition to live up to or to react against. This is the first book-length study of the whole field of New Zealand dramatic literature, and a major problem has been in finding a focus on a fast-developing subject without imposing a rigid authorial pattern. To an extent, the subject is self-defining: any playwright who has been acclaimed by major critics has automatically been considered, even if his achievement seems in retrospect to have been overrated. However, a considerable number of theatrically popular but technically undistinguished playwrights have been ignored, and a few more substantial ones have proved elusive; such is the case of Phillip Mann, who, with a documentary play about Vietnam, a children's play, and a mime script in French, defied coherent analysis.

The forty playwrights whose work is discussed in detail present wide variations in technical complexity, and this is inevitably reflected in critical analysis; if a playwright does not deal in terms of conventional narrative or characterization, criticism must return to a basis in theory. Every attempt has been made to keep theoretical references within the range of the nonspecialist adult reader, but some sections are unavoidably more complex than others. No consideration has been given to mimes, children's plays, or multimedia works that are not primarily dramatic.

From the Notes and References to the text, the reader will observe that the most useful national coverage of contemporary New Zealand drama is found in *Act* (a quarterly until 1975, a monthly bulletin since then) and in *New Zealand Listener* (weekly). It was not feasible to include reviews of individual plays from these sources in the bibliography of criticism, but the reader with access to *Act* will easily find basic data for tracing a play's production history. The publishers of *Act* (P.O. Box 9767, Wellington) form the New Zealand Centre of the International Theatre Institute, coordinating professional theaters and representing playwrights.

HOWARD McNAUGHTON

University of Canterbury

Acknowledgments

The New Zealand University Grants Committee supported my initial research by providing a postgraduate scholarship and several research grants. Professor John Garrett gave the research project valuable encouragement in its early stages. Dr. Bruce Cochrane, Dr. David Carnegie, and Professor D.F. McKenzie made productive comments on early drafts of some chapters. Many playwrights or their representatives have allowed access to manuscript material and have given permission to quote from such sources; chief among these have been Mrs. Jacquie Baxter, Edward Bowman, Eric Bradwell, Alistair Campbell, P.R. Earle, Robert Lord, Dr. Bruce Mason, Playmarket Inc., and Radio New Zealand. For assistance in typing, checking, collating information, scanning newspaper files, and patiently attending a great variety of theater, I am particularly grateful to my wife, Rosemary McNaughton.

Chronology

1840 New Zealand Company settlement of Wellington.

1841 Dramatic performances in Auckland.

1843 Royal Victoria Theatre opened in Wellington by James Marriott.

1848 James Marriott's "Marcilina; Or the Maid of Urnindorpt," the first recorded production of a locally written play.

1861 Gold discovered in Otago.

1862 Two theaters built in Dunedin. B.L. Farjeon and Julius Vogel writing for the Dunedin stage.

1875 Launce Booth's "Crime in the Clouds," Christchurch.

1881 J.C. Williamson company first toured New Zealand.

1882 First New Zealand play published: *Weighed in the Balance* by "Arthur Fonthill" [J.C. Firth].

1887 Dunedin Shakespeare Club founded [survived into 1960s].

1890 *New Zealand Sporting and Dramatic Review* appeared, and continued weekly publication [with title variations] until 1942.

1893 *The Triad*, a controversial monthly, published until 1927.

1895 "The Land of the Moa" by George Leitch, toured New Zealand.

1903 Merton Hodge and Frank Sargeson born.

1911 Allen Curnow born.

1914 *Three Plays for the Australian Stage* by Arthur H. Adams.

1920 *Three Plays of New Zealand.* by Alan Mulgan.

1921 Bruce Mason born.

1925 Alistair Campbell born.

1926 First civic "Repertory" theater established, in Wellington. James K. Baxter and Gordon Dryland born, Eric Bradwell arrived in New Zealand.

1927 *New Zealand Radio Record* began publication.

1929 *Art in New Zealand* established and continued in various forms until 1949.

1932 New Zealand branch of British Drama League established. Peter Bland born.

1933   *The Wind and the Rain* by Merton Hodge began its three-year London run. Alexander Guyan born.

1935   Joseph Musaphia born. Hodge's *Grief Goes Over.*

1936   Bradwell's *Clay.* Mervyn Thompson and Graham Billing born.

1939   *Falls the Shadow* by Ian Hamilton. *New Zealand Listener* founded [incorporating *Radio Record*]. Roger Hall born.

1942   Craig Harrison born.

1943   Ngaio Marsh began series of major Shakespeare productions with Canterbury university students.

1944   Unity Theatre, Wellington, officially founded. Frank Edwards born.

1945   New Zealand Drama Council established. Robert Lord born.

1946   Claude Evans's *The Clock Strikes the Hour,* Christchurch.

1947   Community Arts Service founded, touring productions from Auckland. Dean Parker born. *Landfall* and *New Zealand Theatre* [N.Z. Drama Council monthly] began publication.

1948   First public production of Curnow's *The Axe.*

1949   Jennifer Compton born.

1952   New Zealand Players founded by Richard and Edith Campion.

1953   Mason's "The Bonds of Love" and "The Evening Paper."

1954   Evans's *Overtime.*

1956   Mason's *The Pohutukawa Tree.* Baxter's *Jack Winter's Dream.*

1957   Stella Jones's *The Tree* premiered in Bristol. New Zealand Playwrights Association formed.

1958   Mason's "Birds in the Wilderness." Merton Hodge drowned.

1959   Baxter's *The Wide Open Cage.* Mason's *The End of the Golden Weather.* Curnow's "Moon Section."

1960   New Zealand Players, managed by a trust board since 1956, ceased operations in mid tour.

1961   Globe Theatre, Dunedin, opened under management of Patric and Rosalie Carey. Sargeson's *A Time for Sowing.* Musaphia's *Free.* Television transmissions began in several cities.

1962   Campbell Caldwell's "Flowers Bloom in Summer." Sargeson's *The Cradle and the Egg.* First radio plays of Musaphia and Warren Dibble. Guyan's *Conversations with a Golliwog.*

1963   Campbell's *Sanctuary of Spirits.*

1964   Downstage Theatre, Wellington, founded. Campbell's "The Homecoming." Mason's *Awatea* completed.

1965 Mason's "The Counsels of the Wood," "The Waters of Silence," "Swan Song," "The Hand on the Rail." Dibble's "A Recital." Billing's "Mervyn Gridfern Versus the Baboons."

1966 Baxter, Burns Fellow at University of Otago, wrote "The First Wife," "Mr. Brandywine Chooses a Gravestone." Bland, *Father's Day.* Dibble's *Lines to M* written. Community Arts Service theater ceased operations.

1967 Baxter began series of plays for Globe Theatre. Canterbury Theatre Company established and dissolved. *Act* magazine initiated at Downstage under Mason's editorship. *New Zealand Stage* ceased publication within a year. Max Richards's *The Queue.*

1968 Mercury Theatre, Auckland, opened. Stage premiere of Mason's *Awatea* by Downstage, radio production of *Hongi.* Dryland's "Dark Going Down." Jenny McLeod's "Earth and Sky."

1969 Baxter's "The Day that Flanagan Died." Gulbenkian series of New Zealand plays at Downstage.

1970 Mason's *Zero Inn.* Baxter's *The Temptations of Oedipus.* Four Seasons Theatre, Wanganui, opened. N.Z. Drama Council merged with N.Z. branch of British Drama League to form N.Z. Theatre Federation.

1971 Court Theatre, Christchurch, opened. Amamus Theatre Group and Theatre Action established. Musaphia's *The Guerrilla.* Eve Hughes's *Mr Bones and Mr Jones.* Dryland's *If I Bought Her the Wool.* Lord's *It Isn't Cricket,* "Friendship Centre."

1972 Gateway Players, Tauranga, opened. *Islands,* a quarterly of arts and letters, founded. Taylor's *Digby.* Lord's *Meeting Place, Balance of Payments,* "Moody Tuesday." Thompson's *O! Temperance!* Amamus's "Fifty-one." Death of James K. Baxter.

1973 *Act* incorporated *New Zealand Theatre.* Playmarket formed. McNeill's *The Two Tigers.* McNeish's "The Rocking Cave," the first major production of a New Zealand play at Mercury Theatre. Amamus's "Pictures." Theatre Action's "The Best of All Possible Worlds." Musaphia's *Victims.* New Zealand Playhouse: seven television plays. Fortune Theatre, Dunedin, Theatre Corporate [Co-op], Auckland, founded.

1974 Centrepoint Theatre, Palmerston North, opened. Thompson's *First Return.* Lord's "Well Hung," "Heroes and Butterflies." Banas's "W.A.S.T.E.," "Valdramar." Musaphia's

Obstacles. Harrison's *Tomorrow Will Be a Lovely Day, Ground Level, The Whites of Their Eyes.* Parker's "Smack." New Zealand Playwrights' Conference.

1975   N.Z. Theatre Federation national festival restricted to New Zealand plays. Amamus in Poland. Compton's *Crossfire.* Musaphia's *Mothers and Fathers.* Circa Theatre, Wellington, founded.

1976   Mason's "Not Christmas, but Guy Fawkes," "Courting Blackbird." Edwards's "Bully." Dryland's "Think of Africa," "Fat Little Indians." Thompson's "Songs to Uncle Scrim." Hall's *Glide Time.* Central Theatre, Auckland [founded 1962] closed.

1977   Mason awarded honorary doctorate by Victoria University. Banas's "Package Deal." Amamus's "Song of a Kiwi." Hall's *Middle-Age Spread.* Thompson's "A Night at the Races."

1978   Unity Theatre closed. Edwards's "Pigland Prophet." Hall's *State of the Play,* "Cinderella." Musaphia's "The Hangman." Mason's "Suitcases." Mason's solo performances interrupted by cancer operation.

1979   Feature films of Baxter's *Jack Winter's Dream* and Hall's *Middle-Age Spread.* Musaphia's "Hunting." McNeill's "The Naval Officer." Lord's "High as a Kite." Hall's "Prisoners of Mother England."

CHAPTER 1

The Emergent Drama, 1840–1914

WHEN the systematic colonization of New Zealand began in 1840, the English and Scottish settlers faced a rugged, largely unexplored country. The six early townships were widely separated through the two major islands, and each settlement quickly established cultural idiosyncrasies which were to be fostered by isolation and parochialism. The indigenous Maori population had no theater form of its own, and the European settlers—with a background of Protestant puritanism—were largely antagonistic to the arts. This meant that mid-nineteenth-century New Zealand drama was practiced by an atypical minority, viewed only by the more adventurous of the citizenry, and reported—if at all—by morally defensive newspaper columnists. However, when one considers that one quarter of these early settlers were totally illiterate, and that these seem to have constituted the bulk of the early theater audience, it is easy to accept that colonial New Zealand drama was initially a laboring-class phenomenon which often attracted wider public attention only through the court columns of the newspapers.

I Colonial Production Conditions

By 1843, regular theatrical performances were established in the North Island townships of Auckland and Wellington, and in the South Island settlement of Nelson. In each case, the theater was under the patronage of a popular hotel and catered for an appropriately unsophisticated audience, with farces, melodramas, or variety programs. The scale of these enterprises was not sufficient to generate much lasting publicity, and it may be assumed that numerous similar hotel theaters emerged in most New Zealand settlements within a decade.

Under such production conditions, the literary genesis of a script is of little concern to anyone but the researcher. Claims of novelty and originality were attached even to hackneyed pieces, and the New

Zealand stage probably saw its share of the literary piracy that flourished within nineteenth-century melodrama. The first recorded performance of a locally written play in New Zealand was on July 11, 1848, when James Marriott wrote, produced, and acted a lead part in "Marcilina; Or the Maid of Urnindorpt;"[1] this two-act drama attracted a full house at Wellington's Britannia Saloon, but was neither published, reported, nor revived. Whether this was the first New Zealand play to reach the stage, and whether it was a wholly original work, may not be determined.

In the early colonial period Auckland developed most quickly. Its population was relatively cosmopolitan with a significant Irish element; being in the north, it had the closest link with Australia, and absorbed several pioneers of the Australian stage. However, two developments undermined the presidency of Auckland and increased the cultural importance of Dunedin, in the far south: the Maori Wars and the New Zealand Gold Rushes.

Intermittent warfare with the Maori population was largely the result of disputed land sales, and extended from 1854 until after the withdrawal of the last British troops in 1870. Most of the fighting was in the North Island, and visiting British regiments both dominated theater audiences and presented theatrical entertainments themselves: the identity of the North Island theater was to a considerable extent invested in the troops, and their gradual departure had a sobering effect on many aspects of local life.

Gold was discovered in Otago in 1861, and the population of Dunedin quintupled in two years; by 1863, a quiet Scottish township had developed into a cosmopolitan city of sixty thousand, including many itinerant veterans of the Australian and Californian goldfields. At about the same time, a gold rush led to the settlement of the West Coast of the South Island. The diggers had their own entertainment habits, which led to much of New Zealand's hotel entertainment being transplanted directly to the goldfields. But the influx of wealth also led to the construction of substantial civic theaters in the supporting cities of Dunedin and Christchurch, and to other cultural developments like the establishment of the University of Otago in 1869. Gradually, this educational and theatrical consolidation was to produce the first fully New Zealand playwrights, but many of the early writers who contributed to the emergent New Zealand drama were in no sense New Zealanders; like the goldfields audiences, they were itinerants who happened to work briefly in New Zealand.

George Darrell is usually regarded as an Australian playwright, and as such his work has been adequately discussed.[2] But Darrell was

born in England (in about 1850), and served his theatrical apprentice-
ship in the New Zealand goldfields before establishing himself as an
Australian playwright in 1877 and devoting most of his career to
touring Australia and New Zealand. New Zealand theater columnists
were often unaccountably hostile to Darrell's most successful plays,
such as "Transported for Life" (1877), *The Sunny South* (1883), and
"The Double Event" (1893).

Another playwright whose career spanned the Australasian theater
circuit was George Leitch, whose early work consisted mainly of
stage adaptations of novels, such as *His Natural Life* in 1886 and
Wanda in 1887; in 1895 Leitch wrote "The Land of the Moa," the most
successful nineteenth-century melodrama on a New Zealand subject,
and the only such work surviving in manuscript.

The most illuminating account of the attitudes and conditions of the
itinerant professionals in the period after the gold rushes occurs in Joe
Graham's *An Old Stock-Actor's Memories.* Graham was working in
Christchurch in 1875, when the local theater was managed by
William Hoskins, an eminent veteran of the English and the Australian theater. Graham's account of the Christchurch theater is anecdotal, and it is only while arguing his own involvement in the first
balloon ascent on stage that he mentions "Crime in the Clouds,"
written by Launce Booth, the company's juvenile.

In most respects, "Crime in the Clouds" seems to have been an
undistinguished mid-Victorian melodrama with a narrative structure
similar to that used by George Darrell. The first two acts were set in
Buckinghamshire, and involved a secret marriage between an English aristocrat and his gamekeeper's daughter, with numerous other
interests complicating the relationship. It was in Buckinghamshire
that the balloon was located, but with the third act the drama shifted
to New Zealand:

The author here made his debut in the character of the gallant Major Von
Tempsky, killed in the Waikato War of 1866, and was greeted with a storm of
cheers. A special feature was to have been the introduction of a real native
war-dance—when well done one of the most terribly impressive sights
imaginable—but the Middle Island Maoris are a mild, inoffensive race, vastly
inferior to the fierce, tattooed tribesmen of Auckland or Taranaki, and the
idea was abandoned. We managed, however, to unearth a few dusky supernumeraries from a native "whare" at Kaiapoi, who, in consideration of a
certain small tribute to their head man, and a bottle of rum apiece, conde-
scended to waft a faint air of realism, and a strong odour of fish oil, over the
footlights.[3]

Graham's narrative argues emphatically against a popular notion that
the Maori has until recently been reluctant to appear in drama
because of ancestral doctrine that identity is too sacrosanct to be
tampered with through impersonation or characterization. Maori
actors have always been in short supply on the New Zealand stage,
but not for the reasons commonly given, as Graham's account of the
Maori scene makes clear:

The low comedian, having fallen into the hands of the wily enemy, was,
according to the author, bound to the stake, tortured, and finally set fire to.
This was a serious solecism, inexcusable in anyone who had actually lived in
the country. The New Zealand savage does not, and never did, torture the
captive . . . He would eat him cheerfully, and to that end would tenderly
bake him with an abundance of yams, plantain leaves, and fern root, but his
"long pork" was invariably despatched as quickly and mercifully as possible.[4]

The torture scene obviously appeared purely for formulaic reasons,
as the conventional melodramatic consequence of the aliens temporarily getting the upper hand, whether they were American Indians, Congolese Negroes, or South Sea cannibals. Anthropological
accuracy seems to have troubled neither actors nor audience, and the
Maori supernumeraries allegedly participated in this stage travesty of
their tribal ethos with scarcely controllable enthusiasm.
    Graham and his fellow professionals clearly thought of themselves
as craftsmen rather than as artists; they had no literary interests or
pretensions, and their working conditions did not allow for detailed
interpretation of particular scripts. But at the same period the New
Zealand stage saw the emergence of numerous men of letters who
were as interested in publication as in performance; indeed, none of
the New Zealand plays published before 1900 seems to have reached
performance.

II *Early Literary Playwrights*

    The first of New Zealand's notable literary playwrights was the
novelist B.L. Farjeon, of Dunedin. His three-act melodrama "A
Life's Revenge" (1864) was set in France of the Revolution, and his
burlesques "Faust" (1865) and "Guy Fawkes" (1867) achieved a
modest local popularity. A stage version of Farjeon's goldfields novel
Grif (1867) toured much of the country in 1881.[5]

The first daily newspaper in New Zealand was founded in Dunedin, largely by Julius Vogel, who was later to become one of the country's most celebrated politicians. Under Vogel's patronage literature and the arts flourished in Dunedin, and his own five-act stage version of *Lady Audley's Secret*, which premiered in 1863, was revived for the Duke of Edinburgh's visit in 1869.

Vogel's play was first presented anonymously, a common practice among gentlemen playwrights of the period, and one that has obscured the literary origins of several nineteenth-century New Zealand writers. The most spectacular such case is that of Fergus W. Hume, who became famous in England as the author of more than one hundred detective novels; the most successful of these, *The Mystery of a Hansom Cab* (1886), sold half a million copies. Hume was born in England in 1859 and taken to New Zealand in his infancy; he was educated at Otago Boys' High School and at the University of Otago, and in 1885 he qualified as a New Zealand barrister before leaving for Australia. Hume established himself as a playwright in Dunedin in 1883 with a commedietta "Once Bitten Twice Shy" and a burlesque "Dynamite; or the Crown Jewels." Having suggested that these plays "if criticised at all should be treated at present with all the leniency due to a maiden effort,"[6] the *Otago Witness* critic roundly condemned every aspect of Hume's dramaturgy with a thoroughness that seems unduly harsh. By 1896, Hume was working in Britain and had had some success on the London stage, but he was faring little better critically; William Archer found "The Fool of the Family" devoid of coherence, competence, ingenuity, and common sense, and dismissed Hume's "Teddy's Wives" as "an utterly futile and childish farce."[7]

Despite the consensus of two such critics, Hume's plays cannot be dismissed as insignificant. One of his early pieces, the farcical comedy "The Bigamist," was successful on the New Zealand stage in 1886, and the dramatization of *The Mystery of a Hansom Cab* was very popular in Australasia and ran for five hundred performances at the Princess Theatre, London. In several of his novels Hume wrote of the difficulties facing the colonial playwright in terms that seem highly autobiographical. In particular, *Miss Mephistopheles* (1890) deals with a young man in Melbourne attempting to contrive production for his burlesque "Faust Upset"; in many details, including a general inversion of the characters' sexes, Hume appears to have been echoing Farjeon's "Faust" burlesque, of which he must have heard during his boyhood in Dunedin.

III   *The First Published Plays*

One may trace themes and techniques within early New Zealand drama from secondary sources, but the absence of scripts makes literary evaluation impossible. Between 1880 and 1930 scripts were occasionally published, generally by overseas publishers; it does not follow, however, that these scripts were necessarily typical of the best New Zealand drama of the period.

The first published New Zealand play, Josiah Clifton Firth's *Weighed in the Balance: A Play for the Times*, appeared in 1882 under the pseudonym of Arthur Fonthill. As the title suggests, the play is a political tract full of thinly veiled satirical references to New Zealand politicians; Sir Julius Vogel, for example, appears as "July Vocal." The three acts are spread over three locations: a cavern, a baronial hall, and the Hall of Representatives. Although the character range is considerable, the play's action is minimal, consisting largely of debates on politics and principles of equality. The play obviously contained a good deal of topical allusion which is now only accessible to the historian, but there is no evidence that it made any real impact at the time, political or artistic.

Political satire has always been common on the New Zealand stage. As early as 1855 a playbill attests to a "grand local, legendary, descriptive, subscriptive, serio-comic, mock-heroic, democratical, autocratical *piece de circonstance*" full of topical invective,[8] and the tradition continues with contemporary works like John Banas's "The Robbie Horror Show" (1976). *Weighed in the Balance* is also typical of numerous plays that followed it in its formal, rhetorical language and verse, in its deployment of aristocratic characters and emblems of a kind that has never been prominent in New Zealand, and in its totally unrealistic presentation of indigenous elements, such as the choric witches.

Other playwrights found that a formal, Latinate style was more suited to the treatment of historical subjects. W.H. Guthrie-Smith's *Crispus* (1891) is a three-act, blank-verse drama based on Gibbon. James Izett, a Christchurch journalist, wrote "Terrible Terry" in 1881,[9] a three-act comedy set in Australia that utilized the Ned Kelly scare for its resolution; but Izett's only published play is *King George the Third, A Tragedy* (1899), a complex five-act drama derived from Thackeray's *Four Georges*. Izett's work is distinguished from that of Guthrie-Smith and Firth in that it shows some sense of stagecraft, although of a somewhat archaic nature: the ghosts and mad scenes are used in the manner of Otway, and the indications of formalized focal grouping suggest early Victorian stage style. An extreme example of formal, literary drama on a historical subject is R.T. Hammond's *Under the Shadow of Dread* (1908), a five-act drama in blank verse dealing with King Alfred's conflicts with the Danish invaders; the play's narrative content is unexciting, but the management of archaic dialogue shows a linguistic enterprise that is rare in early New Zealand drama.

Most aspects of Hammond's style now seem absurd or pretentious, but within the historical context of New Zealand literature his achievement was by no means insignificant. Hammond's linguistic competence becomes clear when measured against the dramas of Maurice R. Keesing, published in New Zealand in 1909, but probably written about fifteen years earlier. Keesing also attempted historical drama in *The Destroyers*, and displayed his prowess at languages with various excursions into Russian, pidgin German, and Esperanto; also, Keesing's work did at least reach the New Zealand stage, with "a national and patriotic song and chorus" performed in 1897.[10] But Keesing's attempt to construct a three-act drama on local themes did little more than expose the banality of his literary affectations and a supercilious disregard for the social structure of New Zealand, Maori, and European. *Rotorua: a Fantasy* is located at the famous tourist attractions of the Waitomo Caves and the Rotorua thermal region, and its action culminates with the historical Tarawera eruption. The whole play is in rhyming couplets, and the nature of its cast may be judged from the list of supernumeraries: *"Visiting fairies (Indian, Malay, and Burmese). Gnomes, Giants, Maori Fairies. Tourists. Porters. People of Township. Maoris (in background)."*[11]

Rotorua: A Fantasy is itself little more than an embarrassing literary curiosity of a kind that was not uncommon in the first two decades of this century. But it also anticipates a kind of local formula drama that persisted at least until the 1950s: the audience is invited to view Maori and pakeha (European) behavior through the eyes of on-stage tourists whose inherent curiosity takes them from one natural or social cataclysm to another. The tourist perspective excuses any distortion in the representation of local custom, and conveniently mollifies any audience prejudice that may be consolidated by the play's content. Examples of this kind of play are numerous, and include H.S.B. Ribbands's comedy opera *Marama; or the Mere and the Maori Maid* (1920) and Merton Hodge's "Earthquake" (1931).

IV   The Land of the Moa

Few New Zealand playwrights of the late nineteenth century wrote with book publication in mind. The effective enforcement of copyright laws meant that by 1880 an Australasian production of a recent London or American stage success was a substantial financial investment, and often production rights were withheld if a world tour seemed likely; as early as 1890, for example, the Janet Achurch production of Ibsen's *A Doll's House* was seen throughout New Zealand, although most touring companies were assembled especially for the Australian circuit. These, and related issues, meant that several actor-managers turned playwright themselves or commissioned local work; their general motive was financial, and they compensated for a script's lack of an international reputation by insisting on a plethora of local color. The result was a quantity of plays that were determinedly ephemeral in their impact, sensational theater pieces which reveal a great deal about the social context of New Zealand drama but are themselves of little literary worth.

George Leitch's "The Land of the Moa" (1895) was preeminent among these. The prologue, printed in the program, gave a synopsis of the play's exposition:

The action in the prologue occurs during the period of the Maori war, when the Maoris fought against the English in defence of their tribal rights. The scene is laid in the North Island of New Zealand, in the "Pah" or settlement of Rewi, a highly-esteemed Maori warrior and chief. Rewi is entertaining a Captain Eden, hailing from America, whose plausible manners and a certain reckless daring have excited the admiration and confidence of his savage host, who, up to this time, has had no experience of the wiliness of the white man. Eden not only disposes of his cargo of comparatively useless guns, ammunition, etc., to Rewi, but he betrays his plans of defence and aggression to the English, assisted first by a treacherous Maori named Hangi, and secondly (but unwittingly) by Kura, Rewi's beautiful daughter, the pride of her father and people, whose affections Eden has ensnared, spite of her being betrothed to Roto, the brave young chief of a friendly tribe. In defiance of the warnings of Wangarita, and the mother of Roto, Kura consents to fly with her deceiver. In the effort to prevent their flight Wangarita's husband and Roto's brother are shot down by Eden, who escapes with Kura in his vessel. Over the dead bodies of the slain Rewi, Wangarita, and Roto, their tribes swear an oath of vengeance against the man, whom they ever afterwards dub the Black Angel, Rewi prophesying that he will return to meet his doom at their hands.[12]

All the stock characters of melodrama are here suggested, and the materialization of Rewi's prophecy needs only the introduction of a comic (played by Leitch) and his niece, Marvis Noble. As a story, "The Land of the Moa" is hackneyed, but in terms of technique and moral implications the play has a particular interest.

The morality of nineteenth-century melodrama involved the affirmation of audience norms, often by capitalizing on local racist, nationalistic, or social feelings; thus, it was not uncommon for American melodrama to use a Mexican, Indian, or half-caste villain. The subject of "The Land of the Moa" was colonial warfare, and the final affirmation was patriotic, with the singing of "Rule Britannia." In such a context, one might expect a Maori villain, and yet the Black Angel is emphatically American, while a Maori princess is a heroine. In this respect, the play is typical of New Zealand melodrama: the villains were almost always American or European stereotypes, and Maori characters were generally presented as noble savages sympathetic to the cause of British imperialism. Leitch's manuscript shows that in the first draft Rewi was called "Te Kooti," the name of a historical Maori chief who led guerrilla warfare—including cannibalism and extensive massacres—against European settlers in the years around 1870. The name was fictionalized in the play presumably to veil an unwelcome reality about Maori-pakeha relations. It is also characteristic of the period that Maori supernumeraries were employed for the war dances and group effects, but all the principal Maori parts were played by Europeans. Sociologically, the romanticized portrayal of Maori ethnicity relates to the willingness of Maoris to contribute to its presentation.

The dramaturgic technique of "The Land of the Moa" shows most clearly the influence of the Irish dramatist Dion Boucicault, whose work was widely known through the Australasian touring of Dion Boucicault, Junior, between 1885 and 1896. The climax of the drama lies in a typical sensation scene, at the end of the third act, where the set presents a mountain gorge with a bridge and practical waterfall. The bridge is scheduled for demolition within the hour, but Roto anticipates it, so that the act ends with the direction: " . . . . *a fount of fire seen at back and L of bridge, which is blown up and the horse with Marks* [the Black Angel] *falls into the river below. Water fowl alarmed fly up into the air.*"[13]

Technically, it was necessary for the villain to survive to provide another strong curtain at the end of the fourth act; here, he is shot, blinded with blood from tomahawk blows, dragged to the scene of an eruption, and hurled into a blow hole, "where he is engulphed by a fount of steam and fire."[14] Whether this is the end of the Black Angel, or whether he dies in the course of the eruption that dominates the last act, is uncertain.

It is entirely characteristic of nineteenth-century melodrama that the moral resolution should be effected through natural causation rather than through human endeavor: earthquakes, avalanches, and volcanoes are thought to be in sympathy with Victorian virtue, and all the virtuous need do is let Nature take her course. But in New Zealand, where a tiny population is scattered through a cluster of rugged islands, Nature is relatively a more insistent force than in the densely populated countries from which the pioneers came. For this reason, "Man Alone" has always been a dominant theme in New Zealand prose fiction, and for the same reason Nature may participate in New Zealand stage drama with more plausibility than many Europe-orientated critics will allow.

While "The Land of the Moa" was touring New Zealand, the same audiences also saw Thomas William Robertson's *Caste* and *The Player*, Arthur Wing Pinero's *The Second Mrs. Tanqueray*, *The School Mistress*, *Dandy Dick*, and *The Amazons*, Sutton Vane's *The Span of Life*, William Gillette's *Held by the Enemy*, Henry Arthur Jones's *The Case of Rebellious Susan*, Sydney Grundy's *The New Woman* and *The Village Priest*, and Oscar Wilde's *The Importance of Being Earnest* and *An Ideal Husband*. Very few overseas melodramas were reaching the New Zealand stage; instead, the new drama of social realism was in vogue, a genre in which local playwrights were at a severe disadvantage because of the self-consciousness that seems inevitable in small populations. According to the aesthetic criteria that came through Wilde, Pinero, and even Robertson, "The Land of the Moa" was widely condemned by critics as an old-fashioned pictorial melodrama, dependent on natural spectacle rather than complexity of character interaction.

"The Land of the Moa" used nineteen painted sets, presented on the "grooves" system, which was fast becoming obsolete. At least one canvas was completely repainted for each new theater, with dialogue appropriately adapted, so that the first scene could be located in whichever town the company happened to be playing. The scene of the catastrophe involved the reproduction of a part of Rotorua destroyed in the Tarawera eruption: practical geysers, mud pools, and scenic terraces, facsimiles constructed strongly enough to carry horses. This, however, offended critics less than the sheer quantity of the scenic splendors through which the central action, the pursuit of the villain, passes. The characters caught in the eruption include tourists, the hero and his friend are young Englishmen on a writing and sketching holiday, and in the last scene the characters depart from the New Plymouth wharf, presumably sailing back to England. The whole production could easily be dismissed as an exercise in tourism.

It is absurd to complain, as some critics did, that the characters of the melodrama are undermotivated; the Black Angel careers through Maoriland simply because it is in the nature of melodrama that images of evil be propelled into a context of extreme beauty and innocence. The development of the action simply involves an increasingly intense correlation between the viciousness of the villain and the Romantic savagery of the environment which he exploits. In the theater of 1895 the Black Angel seems to have functioned as a scapegoat for the audience's sense of imperialist guilt, the European characters reflect colonial philanthropy at its most fatuous (with the ship awaiting the end of the South Seas adventure), and the scenic environment explains the lure of the land and its own brand of natural selection. The irony that qualified these central melodramatic fantasies was that the moa—the wingless giant bird of the title—had long been extinct, as obsolete an emblem as the utopian ideals of Rousseau.

V *The Successors to George Leitch*

Of the numerous other New Zealand playwrights who attempted to localize melodrama, the most celebrated is Barrie Marschel. "The Murder at the Octagon" (1895) gave a Dunedin setting to a crime story remarkably similar to Hume's *The Mystery of a Hansom Cab,* and "Humarire Taniwha" (1898) had its blind, part-Maori heroine of the title tied to a Dunedin railway track. For "Crime at Cathedral Square" (1903) Marschel used a Christchurch location, but he then left the stage to work in film distribution, and his play "The Kid from Timaru" was best known in its film version of 1918. Marschel's work remains noteworthy as the epitome of successful stage parochialism, and in the synopses of his plots one notes the importance of French, Corsicans, and other traditional melodramatic nationalities which had little to do with New Zealand.

Marschel's work seems to have been constricted in terms of both scale and budget, but an attempt to match the successes of "The Land of the Moa" came in 1904 from another Australian actor-manager, Alfred Dampier. Dampier and Leitch had long been engaged in rivalry over the stage exploitation of local material (they had each toured a dramatization of *His Natural Life* in 1886), and with "The Growing of the Rata" (1904) Dampier seems to have adapted a play by a young New Zealander, Charles Owen, to suit a wider Australasian audience. In New Zealand, the play was condemned for a lack of motivation and morality, although one suspects that in its presentation of Maori-pakeha miscegenation it was somewhat ahead of its time. For the subsequent Australian tour, the play was rescripted and retitled "The Unseen Hand"; though the production was highly praised for its sensational and scenic effects, the play did not receive a popular or critical response like that of "The Land of the Moa."

In terms of spectacle and exploitation of ethnic detail, the achievement of "The Land of the Moa" was most nearly parallelled by local opera. Maori themes were no novelty in this genre. As early as 1880, a Mr. Griffen of Wanganui had written a musical extravaganza entitled "Hinemoa," for which the *New Zealand Times* predicted a substantial future: "It will form the groundwork of a permanent entertainment, which might be worked successfully throughout the Colonies, one of the principal features being the introduction of a series of panoramic views, illustrating the Middle Island Sounds and the Hot Lakes of the North Island. The dramatic portion of the entertainment has also the advantage of engaging only four principal performers."[15] Though Griffen wrote more for the local stage, "Hinemoa" appears not to have been revived.

In 1893 F.E. Jones's "The Monarch of Utopia" was a sufficiently successful local light opera to achieve revival, but it had clearly been forgotten by 1904, when "Tapu" by Alfred Hill and Arthur H. Adams was promoted as "the first New Zealand opera."[16] Once again, the location was the Rotorua region, with the second act featuring the natural terraces that were destroyed in the Tarawera eruption; into this terrain comes a touring opera company which, finding itself stranded, engages in a vocal drama with the Maori inhabitants. A characteristic review observed that Adams's "plot is incoherent and ridiculous, and smacks less of New Zealand than of the interior of Africa, as known to the artists of the comic journals."[17] Hill's score was considered to be far superior to the libretto, although it was obviously limited by the impossibility of accommodating tribal musical structures within the formal constrictions of European opera, a problem which was resolved only with Jenny McLeod's "Earth and Sky" in 1968.

The Hill-Adams partnership had existed for some years before "Tapu," but for his next opera Hill appears to have succumbed to criticism and used a different librettist: "A Moorish Maid" (1906) was successful enough in Auckland to merit a professional New Zealand tour, although John Birch's script was much criticized, and the principal dramatic highlight of the evening came in "the dance of the hockey girls."[18] Birch continued as a librettist, notably with "The Belle of Cuba" in 1921, while Hill became conductor of New Zealand's first professional symphony orchestra in 1906 and then spent much of his long musical career in Australia.[19]

Adams similarly did his later work in the Australian theater, as literary secretary to J.C. Williamson and editor of the Red Page of *The Bulletin,* Sydney; his determination to become known as an Australian playwright is reflected in the title of his collection, *Three Plays for the Australian Stage* (1914). The plays themselves, however, have general colonial locations which are accommodated easily into the New Zealand context which was their obvious origin. *Galahad Jones* is a comedy derived from Adams's novel of the same title, *Mrs. Pretty and the Premier* is a political comedy which was regarded as "the first New Zealand play to be produced at a West End theatre,"[20] and *The Wasters* is a "modern comedy" about the corruption of a newly rich family.

In his introduction Adams described his unpublished work, which included a "Cromwellian Romantic play," a "modern comedy" with a Maori setting, and a considerable number of one-act plays. In his use of the term "modern comedy" Adams showed himself to be the first New Zealand playwright consciously writing in the wake of Ibsen and Shaw. *The Wasters* presents a successful businessman talking to his wife about his accountant (whom she wants to reinstate to his former position as his partner) and about their son (who prefers gambling to shopkeeping). A subplot develops, but the central drama pivots on issues of blackmail and paternity, with a *scène à faire* that has bitter undertones. The weaknesses of the play lie in its overassertive morality: the power of true love, the liberating force of honesty, and the dangers of pomposity. On the other hand, Adams's humor has a degree of subtlety, and his dialogue shows a concern for realism. Over the next half-century the principal retardant to the emergence of realism in New Zealand drama was the self-consciousness of a small population when confronted with a self-image.

CHAPTER 2

New Zealand Drama between the Wars

IN the period 1918–1939 the general administrative structure of the New Zealand theater underwent a radical transition. Previously, play production had almost always depended on private enterprise, but established managements were undermined by the rise of motion pictures and in 1930 were making a negligible contribution to the New Zealand theater. Typical of the older approach was Rosemary Rees, novelist, actress, and playwright, who toured several productions of her own plays during 1920–21.

As the private company system diminished, local amateur organizations rose in importance. The universities and the Workers' Educational Association promoted a great deal of playwriting and production, as did the civic "repertory" theaters which began to emerge in 1926; but the greatest stimulus came from the establishment of a New Zealand branch of the British Drama League in 1932. These three types of organization gave national coordination to an industry of one-act playwriting which reached considerable intensity after the Depression.

An early indication of the character of the new movement came with the publication in 1920 of *Three Plays of New Zealand* by Alan Mulgan, already a well-known writer. In his preface James Shelley emphasized the sociological basis of Mulgan's one-act plays: " . . . . dramatic value is inseparable from the analysis of social values implied in the action presented . . . . The various human elements which go to the process of colonisation, the re-valuations involved in the struggle between the memory of old traditions and the presence of new conditions, the bitterness which comes from the neglect of the old culture in the transition period before we become conscious of the rise of a new culture, the weak points in the machinery of political representation,—of such indigenous material does Mr. Mulgan make his scenes."[1] Such preoccupations were already familiar in New Zealand prose fiction, but their translation into dramatic terms was impeded by the constrictions of one-act amateur presentation; the problem was essentially quantitative, one of accommodating images of emergent national identity within the modest confines of one-act, one-set, low-budget production.

Two of Mulgan's plays have rural locations, and the plausibility of the action pivots on the assumed magnetic quality of the isolated back-blocks farmhouse which becomes the arena for coincidental meetings and the welding together of a new society. The one-act farmhouse drama continued to rise in popularity until World War II, with numerous playwrights compounding the weaknesses of Mulgan's method by introducing extraneous elements of causation such as floods, droughts, and economic severities, dramatic conveniences which scarcely disguised the dramaturgic problem of making substantial social comment through the one-act medium. Not until the early plays of Bruce Mason, written in 1952–55 and using urban settings, were Professor Shelley's pronouncements fulfilled.

Although the civic repertory theaters flourished during the Depression, the amateur movement did not have the resources to develop its own full-length scripts, so that more ambitious local playwrights moved overseas. Typical of these was Reginald Berkeley, who was educated in New Zealand but wrote all of his major plays after going abroad; though his plays, such as *The White Chateau* (1925), were popular on the New Zealand stage, Berkeley remained essentially an English playwright. Similarly, Austin Strong came to be regarded as an American dramatist.

I *The Plays of Merton Hodge*

A substantially different case was that of Merton Hodge, who moved to Britain only after establishing a local stage reputation and who returned to New Zealand for the last ten years of his life. All three phases of his career—early promise in New Zealand, spectacular success in Britain, complete failure in New Zealand—illustrate the degree to which production conditions have always governed the nature of New Zealand playwriting.

Hodge was born in Gisborne in 1903 and travelled to Britain as a ship's doctor at the age of twenty-eight. His parents had given him a thorough theatrical education, and as a medical student in Dunedin he had scripted, directed, and acted in satirical revues, as well as directing plays by Noel Coward and John Van Druten; he later wrote that it was after reading Van Druten's *Diversion* that he decided to write plays himself.[2] While travelling to England in 1931, he wrote his first full-length script, "Earthquake," a drama of sexual intrigue set within the context of the recent Napier disaster, which brings the fictional element to a conclusion in accordance with the morality of the British "well-made play." "Earthquake," though unproduced, was obviously intended for the commercial theater; it needs five elaborate sets, most of its thirteen characters are on the fringe of the English aristocracy, and its moral tone is closer to that of Henry Arthur Jones's *The Case of Rebellious Susan* (1894) than to Van Druten's *Young Woodley* (1928).

In Hodge's next—and most famous—play the characters are much more humanized, earning their author the journalistic nickname of "The English Chekhov." *The Wind and the Rain*, first produced as "As It Was in the Beginning," is set in Edinburgh, where Hodge briefly worked as a postgraduate medical student; however, it was clear even to a Paris critic that it was based on experiences in New Zealand.[3] The play involves a group of medical students who share lodgings, and it follows their ambitions and passions over a five-year period; the main character (Charles Tritton) splits his loyalty among three women, his mother, a sculptress, and a childhood sweetheart. After a short, successful trial run in London, Hodge met Van Druten and explained to him that "Charles Tritton is really Young Woodley grown up"; Van Druten suggested how the play should be rewritten before its West End production, and on his advice the whole action was confined to a single set in Edinburgh.

The Wind and the Rain ran for three years in London and was also a commercial success in New York, Paris, Berlin, and numerous other cities; for three months in 1935 it was running simultaneously in London with another of Hodge's plays, *Grief Goes Over*, in adjoining Shaftesbury Avenue theaters. *The Wind and the Rain* illustrates an obsession with decorum that had characterized the British "well-made play"; one critic complained that "it suffered from a solemnity that seemed out of date."[4] Compared with Young Woodley, Charles Tritton is sexually unenterprising, and no character appears as a transgressor against society. Many critics complained of the slightness of the play's action: "Beyond reiterating the platitude that love is greater than sex Mr. Hodge has little to say. His humour is redolent of the dissecting room. It has that flippancy which medical students affect when they are affected by the tragedies of the operating theatre."[5]

Paucity of action is a charge that could not be levelled at *Grief Goes Over*, which involves a dignified London widow, Blanche Oldham, and her three sons, David, Tony, and Kim. Tony is a drug addict who is having an affair with a sailor's wife, and the first act ends with news that he has been shot; in the second act, Mary Lou, a family protegée, becomes pregnant to Kim, giving Blanche a few months to adjust to circumstances before Mary Lou dies in childbirth. A final scene a year later shows Blanche and Kim gradually overcoming their grief. Though sensational in content, *Grief Goes Over* was conservative in its moral implications, illustrating the "well-made" principle that the impure have no right to exist;[6] the addict, the adulterer, and the fallen woman are purged from society, Kim is punished with a grief that outlives that of his mother, and the secondary characters, whose inertia echoes that of *The Wind and the Rain*, are alone vindicated. As in "Earthquake," the play's essential causation is only tenuously related to the dramatized action; Tony's fate dominates the first act, but the specific causes of his death are his drugs, his non-appearing mistress, and the completely anonymous sailor who shoots them. Mary Lou's death in childbirth is simply a blind stroke of fate.

In Hodge's next play, *The Island* (1937), the crisis is similarly precipitated, by the death of an officer's wife in an undramatized mental home, a woman who is completely unknown to every other character. But in all other respects this play generates its own dramatic energy economically and inevitably, creating an intense, claustrophobic atmosphere that gives some basis to the comparison with Chekhov. *The Island* was based on Hodge's experiences in a military hospital at Spike Island, Southern Ireland, and involves nine officers and their wives; the strain of confinement mounts until, in the third act, latent tensions become explicit, and there is a suicide. The effort to maintain society's decorum in a most unfavorable environment explodes toward the end, leaving the survivors to entrench themselves in social norms again. In fact, nothing has been solved and the situation seems likely to recur whenever people attempt to perpetuate English social etiquette in inhospitable surroundings. But the "well-made" play must assert that etiquette in defiance of the environment, and in *The Island* this is largely achieved by the fusion of social and military decorum.

It is one of the numerous ironies of Hodge's career that, had *The Island* been located in New Zealand, it would easily have been accepted as the first classic of New Zealand dramatic realism. But in 1937 Hodge was concerned almost exclusively with London's West End; actresses like Marie Tempest and Sybil Thorndike (who created Blanche) were at his disposal, and he turned increasingly to large-scale dramatizations of novels (such as *The Story of an African Farm* by Olive Schreiner in 1938) and to historical pageants, including "Empress Dowager." When his London success expired and he returned to New Zealand after the War, he had become a theatrical obsoletism, of little relevance to the new production conditions with their emphasis on intimacy. Shortly before his death in 1958, Hodge submitted "Empress Dowager" to Patric Carey in Dunedin: a play covering sixty-three years of Chinese history, demanding seven lavish sets and at least forty characters as well as a host of acrobats, jugglers, and dancers, offered to a director planning a tiny studio theater.

II Eric Bradwell and the Early Influence of Radio

With social realism limited at one-act level, and with Hodge's success orientating the full-length playwright overseas, the most promising area of indigenous advance was the short stylized play. By the Depression period the highest achievement of this kind had been the fantasies and folk plays of C.R. Allen, mostly written in archaic blank verse for English production, intended as contributions to the "drama of ideas." A decade later New Zealand drama had its own works of sophisticated expressionism which were popular with audiences and eminently manageable on the amateur stage. Among several influences that contributed to this development, the most important was radio, which taught playwrights new principles of dramatic chronology and location; Eric Bradwell, the best of these authors, was "strongly influenced in a vague sort of way by the flexibility of radio drama, and was trying to apply the same flexibility to the stage play."[7]

Bradwell was a prominent entrant in early British Drama League competitions with short, "well-made" plays in which he attempted to disguise the coincidental nature of their mechanistic structure by a veneer of realism. In one of these, *Fantasy by Firelight,* he moved slightly outside the confines of drawing room drama, but did not use the technique of dramatized fantasy for anything more than the representation of abstract calculation. In *Clay,* however, Bradwell applied radio techniques, with an abstract set defining two acting areas, and the stage presided over by an almost motionless, unspeaking female figure whose *"whole attitude is one of utter despair."* On one side of the stage is a gray mound, *"as if it has been roughly modelled in clay,"* populated by five creatures who *"represent the woman's mind, and utter the incoherent and fleeting thoughts that are tormenting her.*"[8] For the main body of the play, the action alternates between the right-hand side of the stage, where a stereotyped romantic story is presented episodically, and the left-hand side, where the creatures make semi-articulate noises. At the end of the play, the woman makes her only real contribution to the action: *"Black-out. The figure of the woman suddenly stands and utters a shriek, shielding her eyes from some sight that is too terrible to witness . . . . The woman slowly sinks down again, buries her face in her hands once more, and becomes quite still."*[9]

The rationale of such drama derives ultimately from the Swedish dramatist August Strindberg's preface to *A Dream Play*, principles which Bradwell must have known from numerous intermediary illustrations from the stage of the 1920s. Even if their application in *Clay* had been totally derivative, the play would still have been of extraordinary interest within New Zealand stage history; but *Clay* has a unique importance for the way it generates a contrapuntal tension between those areas of the memory that the dreamer dare not articulate and the areas that have become overfamiliar and are thus reduced to a cartoon-like simplicity. The story element represents an attempted escape into naive rationalization. Stephen persuades Lona, a promising young sculptress, to marry him, even though she insists she does not love him; subsequent scenes show Lona progressing as a sculptress, Stephen visiting her on leave from World War I, and Lona flirting with Carl, a young Belgian. Stephen is blinded, Carl is shot as a spy, Lona discovers she is pregnant; in Scene Eight, eight years have passed, and Stephen has recovered his sight sufficiently to be irritated by a bust of Carl, whom he never knew. In the final scene the striking similarity between Lona's son (now nineteen) and Carl's bust precipitates a crisis, and Lona in her desperation finally gives herself away; at the end of the play, the identity of Lona explicitly merges with that of the Woman.

The resolution of *Clay* simply involves the Strindbergian method of emerging from the dream into a reality which, though agonizing, is obviously less painful than the unspecified immediate consequences of the dream narrative. But the internal linking of the play is novel, generally without the associative coherence normal in psychoexpressionism; the causal connection between the clearly defined story episodes commands the most intense focus, the blurred transitional passages where the choric fragments of the woman's mind take control. From the start, the five creatures immediately establish a dominant rhythmic background to the action: *"The murmuring develops*

*into a loud rhythmic jabbering, from which . . . . sharp staccato
utterances emerge.*"[10] The whole element of causation has been
invested in five nebulous creatures who manipulate the woman into
painful memories and whose general tone is antagonistic to her. Only
one of the creatures is even vaguely individualized, and their utterances, sentence fragments and phatic chants, are accompanied by
musical directions, so that there is an overwhelming sense of group
solidity directed against the woman's solitariness. Every decision-
making situation is preceded by a division among them; generally,
one creature takes an attitude that is empathetic to the woman's
present state of self-pity, while the others attack from an opposite
quarter and determinedly suppress the element of sympathy.
Strindbergian "agony" comes partly because the woman's most intimate defenses are systematically exposed and ruined, and partly
because the machinery for that exposure is so banal and unsympathe-
tic. The annihilatory power of the chorus, in spite of its arbitrary
appearance, leaves the impression that it can find fresh areas for
devastation wherever it turns within the woman's mind; often there is
uncertainty about how each episode is generated, whether the creatures make each scene crystallize just so that they may wreck it, or
whether they let the woman's memory have free rein, confident in
their own power to demolish whatever it produces. In either case,
they are triumphant at the end. As the woman utters her final shriek,
the voices of the chorus fade out in *"a mocking, derisive chuckle."*[11]

Bradwell's achievement in *Clay* was the most significant technical
advance in all pre-World War II New Zealand drama, anticipating the
convergence of radio and stage techniques which was to distinguish
much New Zealand drama in the 1960s. The premiere of *Clay*, in the
Wellington Concert Chamber on April 10, 1936, drew considerable
publicity, even a newspaper editorial. The deliberate blurring of the
play's logical coherence means that it has not suffered the psychological obsolescence which has overtaken many early expressionistic
plays, and *Clay* is the only New Zealand play of its decade to have
been successfully revived in the 1970s.

It was only after he wrote *Clay* that Bradwell began working for
New Zealand radio; later, he became a journalist and received considerable recognition as a drama critic, mainly for the *New Zealand
Listener.* In his radio period he wrote numerous scripts of a semi-
dramatic nature but gradually stopped writing plays because of a
difficulty in finding plots. Only one of Bradwell's radio plays seems to
have survived. "The Last Station" was written privately and entered

in what was probably the first radio playwriting competition in New Zealand, in 1937; unsuccessful there, it was bought and produced by the British Broadcasting Corporation in 1939, and Bradwell himself produced it for the New Zealand commercial radio service a few months later. It seems very likely that this was the first play ever to be produced over New Zealand commercial radio; it is obvious that the technicians were totally inexperienced.

The essential idea of "The Last Station" was taken from a story by Tyrone Guthrie. Bradwell has described how the play's story emerged: "It was the story of two people who had never met who each had recurring dreams. Their dreams mesh in each other's minds. Finally they do meet, and the thing ties up in one episode which is a bush fire on the main trunk." The play attempts to exploit dramatic and psychic predestination by telepathic means; as in *Clay*, Bradwell establishes a rhythmic background that gives the play a dominant air of inevitability. However, the mechanics of relating two dreamers—independent yet complementary—posed insuperable complexities, and Bradwell resorted to an Announcer who explains that "This is the story of two people whose destinies were so interwoven that it seemed that everything happening to them was not coincidence, but a necessary thread in a pattern of existence already pre-conceived."[12] The determinant of the dramatic action is Destiny; although the play has a strong, linear intensification that reveals a keen sensitivity to radio production conditions, its structure seems crude when analyzed as a script, with direct, retrospective narration draining most of the vitality out of the hallucinatory element.

III   *The Expressionistic Plays of J.A.S. Coppard*

The only other New Zealand writer to produce a body of competent expressionistic drama during the 1930s was J.A.S. Coppard, who was born in Taranaki and had a university education in Auckland. Though none of his published plays could rank alongside *Clay* in terms of expressionistic resourcefulness, Coppard wrote more such plays over a much longer productive career than Bradwell; he was obviously very widely read in dramatic literature, and his plays, though remarkably even in quality, generally reveal a derivative basis. This is well illustrated in his first successful play, *Sordid Story*, which made an impressive impact at its premiere at the Scottish Drama Festival in 1932, but which exploits a great deal of presentational detail that was fashionable in the late 1920s. This is evident even in the directions for the setting, which is *"intended to convey the impression of a living cranium into which the audience is looking."* The play's representational technology is complex, requiring a panoply of levers, dials, and flashing lights, so that *"During the whole course of the play the intensity and speed of fluctuation of the heart light in the centre of the 'control' panel are varied with the action. It is intended to represent the record in the brain of the heart's action."*[13] These devices are closely parallelled in the New Zealander Austin Strong's *A Play Without a Name*, which premiered on Broadway in 1928, and in turn derived from Nikolai Evreinof's *The Theatre of the Soul*, which premiered in the West in 1915. The population of Coppard's setting consists of the Eye, the Ear, the Memory, Jealousy, Anger, and the Operator (representing "Reason" or "Soul"), and the play's most serious weakness is that the contents of the colossal cranium turn out to be so trivial; since all these faculties belong to a *"a back-street city type, devoid of any of the finer instincts or feelings,"*[14] the expressionistic subdivision of the cranium is so precise as to make the interplay of the faculties thoroughly banal. Like *Clay*, *Sordid Story* has a simplistic narrative line, involving the apparent murder of the delinquent's unfaithful girlfriend, but Bradwell was able to exploit a tension between the past and the present in a way that Coppard's use of Memory precludes; the vagueness of Bradwell's creatures suggests much more complex mental processes than the few, clearly defined functions of Coppard's cranium admit, and the live commentary narrative of *Sordid Story* fails to generate any of the pathetic inadequacy of the dramatized mind to cope with events, a pathos which is very strong in *Clay*.

For *Machine Song*, which also dates to the mid-1930s, Coppard moved even closer to the core of American expressionism a decade earlier. The scene is a factory, *"any factory or machine shop, where men toil to serve the machines they have made to serve themselves. The keynote of the play is that service of man the slave to his master the machine—its tempo beats throughout the lines."*[15] This could have served as an introductory statement to dozens of plays in the period after World War I, when German expressionism popularized the theme of man-versus-machine and American playwrights followed Elmer Rice in the field. There is little in *Machine Song* that is not parallelled in Rice's *The Adding Machine* (1923); most of the play occurs in the mind of Joe Smith, with the action generated by the Voice of the Machine, a barmaid, an Angel who describes the factory worker's heaven, a policeman, a machine-smashing rebel, and the ghost of an old machine worker. Despite Joe Smith's generic name and stage directions echoing Rice's principle of the slave psychology, *Machine Song* remains one man's subjective drama without any effective presentation of an evolutionary system that creates machine slaves.

Both *Machine Song* and *Sordid Story* are limited because too much of the action hinges on an unresourceful mind at their core. In *The Axe and the Oak Tree,* there is no human factor at all; the participants in this ecological verse drama are the Axe, the Spirit of the tree, various natural forces, and a chorus of twenty-seven voices, the total effect being just a symbolic voice exercise. Coppard continued experimenting with short stylized plays after World War II, and in his last published play, *Candy Pink,* he successfully combined semirealistic and expressionistic elements in a portrayal of a delinquent girl; the play is neither subtle nor stylistically sophisticated, but it does integrate the protagonist's subjectivity with an objective social context, overcoming a limitation of Coppard's earlier work.

The expressionistic plays of Bradwell, Coppard, and a few other writers do not constitute a substantial corpus within New Zealand drama. But their plays do represent a very significant tendency that parallels the work of fiction writers like Frank Sargeson in the 1930s, and that anticipates a major development in New Zealand drama in the 1960s. Many of the central characters in Sargeson's early stories are inarticulate introverts, severely limited in human contact skills and living sheltered, constricted lives in the country; such characters, it has been recognized, reflect a then-common national type. However, it is also obvious that such characters cannot easily be accommodated within the stage realism of Alan Mulgan or the well-made patterning of Merton Hodge. The objectification of inner experience was a seminal purpose of the Expressionist movement, which thus offered a channel for self-representation to a shy, puritanical society searching for integration.

CHAPTER 3

The Development of Poetic and Realistic Drama

WORLD War II altered the character of most New Zealand theaters, changing the nature of the active membership but generally not reducing it. Unbalanced resources led to a period of conservatism in the larger civic theaters and a consequent resistance to local scripts, but the war years also saw a substantial development in university drama and the emergence of socially committed theaters in Wellington and Auckland. At Canterbury University College, Ngaio Marsh directed a series of celebrated productions, mostly Shakespearean, and at Auckland University College Arnold Goodwin developed a marionette theater which also toured Shakespeare productions.

It is almost inevitable that a literary theater movement such as Ngaio Marsh encouraged at Canterbury, stressing voice and stylization, should produce its own original works. The establishment of the Caxton Press had temporarily given Christchurch the highest density of poets in the country, and most of them were involved in the theater. Here James K. Baxter got his first experience of the stage, in Ngaio Marsh's production of Jean-Paul Sartre's *Les Mouches* in 1948, and he was immediately stimulated into beginning his own first play; in this he was also partly following the example of established writers like Sargeson, R.A.K. Mason, Charles Brasch, Allen Curnow, and D'Arcy Cresswell, all of whom had then attempted dramatic writing.

John Pocock, actor and director for the Canterbury University College Little Theatre, considered the period between 1943 and 1948 to be a "small but unmistakable Golden Age" which taught "a training in rhetoric and poetry as the principal means of theatrical expression." He has described the group's priorities: a tendency to regard every script, whether prose or verse, as "a formal pattern of speech," scorn for the "problem play," and an insistence on plays "uncommitted to realism or the contemporary scene." The tradition, in Pocock's

38

view, culminated with the production of Allen Curnow's *The Axe* in 1948, a poetic drama which "provided the actors with some richly satisfying moments of dramatic utterance, closely linked with some of the central ideas in New Zealand poetry at that time"; the production "consisted essentially in the discovery of how potent the great poetic images, the rhythms and melodies of verse, can be in the creation of purely theatrical experience."[1]

I *Allen Curnow's* The Axe

Curnow was one of the senior members of the Caxton group of Christchurch poets, and *The Axe* was an extension of themes and techniques that were already well known from his poetry. *Not in Narrow Seas* (1939) had shown his interest in Polynesian historical material, with an alternation of prose and verse approaching a coherent story-line and one section written in verse dialogue. *Island and Time* (1941) used verse monologues and dialogues involving abstract or superhuman personae, confrontations between elemental forces which were to provide the basis of *The Axe.*

The specific narrative source of *The Axe* was a Yale University lecture delivered by Sir Peter Buck; the subject was Polynesian anthropology (in particular that of Mangaia, in the Cook Islands), and Curnow adhered closley to Buck's details, even using the same names. Buck's account of Mangaia reads:

It had so happened that in the last year the combined tribes of Ngati-tane and Ngati-manahune had defeated the existing government of Ngati-vara . . . . The highest ranking chief was Numangatini, holding the offices of both Inland-high-priest and Shore-high-priest. It was at this peculiar stage that the two Tahitian missionaries landed on Mangaia and came under the protection of the dominant Ngati-tane tribe. In the course of time they made converts . . . . The national god house was burnt to the ground, and the gods that had reposed in it were thrown in a heap before the missionaries . . . . Matters reached a head when the Ngati-vara assembled their forces and offered battle to regain government over the island. . . . During the battle, the Tahitian missionary, Davida, remained on his knees, supplicating Jehovah to grant victory to the Ngati-tane; in a thatched hut perched on a high rock, Tereavai, priest of the Ngati-vara, invoked his tribal god Te A'ia to give success to their arms. The spiritual power of Te A'ia, however, had departed with that of the other Polynesian gods, and the heathen were defeated.[2]

To Buck's narrative, Curnow added a romantic subplot between a youth, Hema, and a girl, Hina; he changed the ending to intensify the tragedy; and he introduced the axe motif. The play is set in various locations around the island, but it was written specially for a single utility set; in its final published version, it is in three acts with a total of eleven scenes, though the first version to be performed consisted of only two acts.

The central symbolism lies in the axe motif, representing imported culture, and it is inevitably used as the instrument of tragic death at the end. The axe also provides some justification for the subplot: it is Hema who receives the axe from the missionary, it is he who loses it to the Ngati-vara, and Hina is one of those killed by it in the last act. It is obviously important that such a basic tool should be seen in use among ordinary people, and the love relationship also illustrates Davida's (historical) "blue laws" restricting sexual freedom. From the first production, however, there was dissatisfaction with the axe symbolism, expressed most succinctly by A.W. Stockwell:

The second dramatic climax occurs in a scene which is the core of the play's meaning, since in it the full significance of the axe's symbolism is revealed concretely, in terms of individual human experience. Hema discovers the girl's corpse—and beside it, the fatal weapon. He renounces Christianity. Crazed by grief and disgust he determines on revenge; he imagines himself a god. Seizing the axe, he rushes out to find Numangatini, who dies after a fight off-stage in the final scene. Hema enters and throws the axe down over the dead body. . . . the symbolism of Hema's axe is unconvincing and incapable of sustaining the weight placed upon it. As a result the whole play seems hollow, both on the printed page and in the theatre.[3]

M. K. Joseph also found the axe motif "self-conscious," but expressed more satisfaction in another area of symbolism: "another image, that of the island, emerges with considerable power . . . . With its cliff and mountain, spray and seaswell, cavern and cloud, it rings solid. And it further suggests a unity of existence which is somehow detached from both the Christians and the pagans."[4] James K. Baxter, who had been at the premiere with Denis Glover, argued vehemently in the play's defense as "a situation archetypal for the Polynesian and for us."[5] Selecting The Axe as one of the five most important events in recent New Zealand poetry, Baxter argued an Edenic interpretation, but without amply refuting the attacks on the symbolism and the quality of the nonchoric verse.

Curnow's concern was for the articulation of Pacific archetypes, and his characterization was no more individualized than is necessary in mythic drama. He gave the best poetry in the play to the chorus of two ancestral voices which begins the play and ends each act, and he extended the chorus's function considerably after the first production. It is in the chorus that the deepest significance of the axe is invested, and the fact that this significance is generally inaccessible to the characters but transparent to the audience means that the play is weighted by a rather obvious irony; this is a fundamental problem when a playwright's purpose lies in the elaboration, rather than the revaluation, of mythic sources. However, in the final version the chorus, with its privileged vision of both past and future, shifts the focus from the individual to the universal, from character interaction to superhuman manipulation by the elemental forces which have chosen these characters as pawns in their primordial conflict.

When reduced to its thematic essence, the conflict of *The Axe* is not among the particular humans but between the abstract figures of Curnow's earlier poetic dialogue, Island and Time. These forces are collated not only by the ethnic convergence of the play's story-line, but also by a mythic motif that recurs in numerous Pacific cultures: that of the island being eternally bound to the seabed, tied there by a god-figure like the Maori Maui. Curnow's axe is not simply—or even primarily—the instrument of a tribal melodrama; it is the unwelcome liberator of the Island into Time.

II *D'Arcy Cresswell's* The Forest

Apart from R.A.K. Mason, whose propagandist sketches are of little theatrical or literary significance, and Charles Brasch, whose *The Quest* is a poetic script for a mime play, the only other New Zealand poet writing seriously for the stage in the 1940s was D'Arcy Cresswell. Although Cresswell's *The Forest* was not published until 1952, a first draft was done in 1936.

As in *The Axe*, *The Forest* involves two elemental forces settling on an obscure Pacific location for a duel; here it is scientific progress versus Nature, the materialist against the poet. Cresswell's battle with Copernicus occupied much of his writing career and often resulted in a forthright dogmatism which is sharply at odds with the sense of comic strategy revealed in *The Forest*. The main character is Mr. Salter, who owns a large area of forest which he is under pressure to sell; in the first version, Salter held the stage from beginning to end and was apparently entrusted with a good deal of authorial pronouncement, derived autobiographically from Cresswell's work for the Forestry Department.

In its final form the play begins with a dialogue between the archangel Gabriel and the restored archangel Lucifer; following a compromise between heaven and hell, Lucifer now controls the earth, particularly through the forces of Science. Gabriel's posture is the first to be punctured: from the start he appears as a superannuated archangel with all the attributes of senility, and it soon becomes clear that his heavenly preoccupations have left him completely out of touch with the power of Nature. Lucifer is altogether a more vital character, but he reveals a dangerous arrogance in his contempt for poets. Since no poet has yet appeared, attention turns to the absent Salter, "a forest Romeo/whose Juliet's his trees,"[6] and Salter's wife, whose attitude to the forest parallels Lucifer's. Taking off his cloak of invisibility, Lucifer becomes Bishop, a fast-talking businessman; Gabriel, who cannot get rid of his invisibility, finds himself hovering helplessly on the fringe of the action. As Lucifer begins to make progress with the wife, the arrival of the Salter's son, Clive, introduces a new dimension, implicitly homosexual, which confuses Lucifer. Salter's own first entrance, delayed until well into the second act, is thus given a context of some moral and strategic complexity, and he seems on the verge of selling his forest. At the start of the final act Gabriel is in conversation with Clive's friend George, who—being a poet—has no difficulty in penetrating the invisibility. George persuades Salter not to sacrifice his forest, Lucifer retires, thwarted by the power of the poet, Bishop dies, and Gabriel decides to stay on earth, throwing off his robe, *"revealing figure of a beautiful young man, naked save for a girdle."*[7]

The Forest is a modest—but significant—achievement. Its verse is of a much lower poetic intensity than Curnow's, but of a higher theatrical cohesiveness; it was specially written for playing rather than reading, although production was delayed until 1963, three years after Cresswell's death. Cresswell's surviving dramatic fragments show that he did attempt tragedy and historical drama, but the basis of his success in *The Forest* lay in choosing the mode of light, literary comedy, without any necessary repercussions outside the animated context. The lightness of tone and audacity of conception were rare in an emergent dramatic literature which was often obsessed with seriousness.

III   *The Plays of Ian Hamilton and Howard Wadman*

Of New Zealand's socially committed theaters, the best-known was Unity Theatre, Wellington, which in the 1940s relied on overseas scripts for its full-length productions. In Auckland, the People's Theatre, deriving from the Workers' Educational Association, produced several of R.A.K. Mason's sketches and also conducted playwriting competitions; the most notable product of these was Ian Hamilton's *Falls the Shadow* (1939), a three-act antiwar drama set in contemporary Britain. Until nearly the end of the second act, the play closely resembles the tradition of the British "well-made play," involving an upper-middle-class family in various domestic and romantic situations in a country house near an airfield on the brink of war. But as the warning siren sounds. the realistic illusion is dropped and a spotlight picks out a recruiting officer, a politician, a strike leader, a strike breaker, and a padre, each arguing a different attitude to the war. In the final act, a year has passed since the English victory, and the country is under the control of its own breed of military fascists who have emerged from the war.

The play ends on a cautious note of optimism and regeneration similar to that of much German expressionism twenty years earlier, but the ending is not eased by any conventional domestic resolution, such as one might have expected from the first act; the family has been shattered morally and physically, and is under surveillance by the fascists. Even the heavily conventional areas of *Falls the Shadow* are interestingly written, the central characters are well developed, and the final act is highly atmospheric even when divorced from the propagandist implications of its prewar context. But perhaps the play's most notable technical feature is its prefatorial "Monologue," spoken by the playwright to a recalcitrant actor, crystallizing the play's propagandist drift in a vernacular style similar to Sargeson's:

. . . . *So what are you going to do after that? The workers'd take control. Yes, but which workers? The best bashers, I suppose. But then don't good bashers make bad bosses. I mean there'll have to be a boss around somewhere. Wait and see? But Christ, Andy, I reckon I CAN see. After all, Hitler's a pretty good basher . . . .*

Well, let's leave that, Andy. The thing I really want to know is, what made you take a part in the play? You took it damn well, I'll admit, damn well. But there's a terrible big gap between getting up on a soap box in Quay Street and telling the chaps what's coming to them if they don't revolute, and this play, isn't there? I must say I wouldn't have the guts to get up on a soap box in Quay Street, and p'r'aps that's why I wrote the play. There's good stuff in it? Yes but the theme, Andy, the theme. It might make the chaps realise what'll happen, if they don't get up and bash the bosses? . . . .[8]

Falls the Shadow is New Zealand's *Waiting for Lefty*, though without any suggestion of stylistic plagiarism; it is a vigorous, iconoclastic piece which allows a rare insight into the workings of an ephemeral and largely nonliterary movement in New Zealand.

The uncommitted civic theaters, by contrast, relied almost exclusively on imported scripts such as the wartime plays of Emlyn Williams. After the war, however, several new playwrights emerged through these societies. In Wellington, Howard Wadman, (editor of *The Year Book of the Arts in New Zealand*) had written his "modern morality play" *Youth Wants to Know* for the Religious Drama Society during the war, and followed it with the more popular *Life Sentence* which received its premiere in Wellington in 1949 amid considerable public attention. *Life Sentence* has a New Zealand setting, and attempts to deal with the problems of national integration within an immediate context of romantic rivalry and mountaineering adventure; in all other respects it is a thoroughly conventional British "well-made play" until in the last act—as in *Falls the Shadow*—the structural constrictions dissolve to admit the presentation of a complex moral issue. *Life Sentence* is technically a clumsy play, with banal characterization, a crude story-line, and pretentious stylistic effects like the use of a verse-speaking ghost in the last act. One of its epigraphs, from T.S. Eliot, indicates an obvious influence, but the other reveals a writer keenly sensitive to the mood of New Zealand audiences: a quotation from James K. Baxter emphasizes that Wadman was aware of issues that were to become dominant in New Zealand drama within a decade, although he lacked the skills with which Baxter and Bruce Mason would articulate them.

IV   *The Plays of Claude Evans*

While Hamilton and Wadman were writing largely for specialist purposes, a more pragmatic South Island playwright was emerging as an astute judge of audience tastes and performance resources. All of Claude Evans's nine full-length plays require elaborate interior sets and large casts of characters who mostly approximate to stock types: scripts carefully gauged to the needs and abilities of the flourishing Christchurch amateur theater. Evans's first four plays were produced in the 1940s, three of them under the direction of Neta Neale, and have several sets, all with a British location. His later plays have a single set, a New Zealand location, and a refinement of characterization; Neta Neale had become committed to the establishment of the Canterbury Children's Theatre, and these plays were mounted with the support of the Canterbury Repertory Theatre.

Of the early works, *The Clock Strikes the Hour* (1946) follows the career of a modern Faustian adventurer in the business world, *Underwood* (1947) is a family saga reflecting the action of a ballet and covering the conflicting emotional demands on its colorless central character over a period of thirty-five years, *There'll Be a Spring* (1948) is a sentimental drama on the theme of scientific rejuvenation, suggesting the influence of Emlyn Williams, and *Far Journey* (1949) is a memory play about the war in China in 1938.

That Man Harlington (1952), Evans's first play with a New Zealand location, is also his first to depend wholly on realistic causation; the stereotyped situation of an embezzling lawyer is augmented by a comical dimension and by careful portraiture of the title character. In *Overtime* (1954) the arena shifts to a furniture factory and the comedy arises from pressures of modernization and unionism; this is Evans's most successful and original play, making a topical impact at its premiere and admitting a greater breadth of characterization than any of his other works. Evans's later plays consist of the atmospheric business drama *Rich Man, Poor Man* (1956), a social comedy about the originally French settlement of Akaroa *So Laughs the Wind* (1958), and a "play of law" set in a Supreme Court, "My Learned Friend" (1961). Like his master Emlyn Williams or his compatriot Merton Hodge, Claude Evans ironically refined a style just as it was beginning to appear dated. Williams, of course, diversified into another theatrical style, a development which was also felt in New Zealand, in the initial influence on Bruce Mason.

CHAPTER 4

The Plays of Bruce Mason

I N 1942, when the "Golden Age" of Shakespeare production was emerging at Canterbury University College, an important new theater with radically different aims appeared in Wellington. Initially, Unity Theatre was committed to the exploitation of the theater for Socialist purposes, and its first productions were "crude propaganda plays," but after the war its membership and program became more eclectic, though its production record until its demise in 1978 indicates that it retained a strong preference for plays with social significance.[1]

I The Early Realistic Plays

In its early years Unity encouraged several one-act playwrights such as Kathleen Ross (*The Trap*, 1950) and Marie Bullock ("Cupid and Psyche," 1950), neither of whom diverged significantly from the national one-act repertoire already established by playwrights like the prolific Isobel Andrews (*The Willing Horse*, 1941). But with Bruce Mason Unity found a writer with the talent and audacity to confront national complacencies skillfully and force a reaction from audiences attuned to West End pleasantries. The title of Mason's first play, "The Bonds of Love" (1953), derives from the second line of the New Zealand national song: "God of nations, at thy feet,/in the bonds of love we meet. . . ." With heavy irony, Mason interprets the bondage sexually, and strategically undermines much of the then-legendary vision of New Zealand as the egalitarian utopia of the South Seas.

The origins of the play were closely researched observations of impoverished local life, condensed into the characters of two immigrant sisters and their boorish men (one a husband, the other a barman). The faintly residual optimism of the women is set against the insensitive pragmatism of the men, and the foursome looks like yielding to a mutual tolerance and sympathy, but reaffirms the uncompromising rigidity of its characters at the end. As a distillation of principles of national and domestic cohesion, "The Bonds of Love" is a work of deep pessimism, compounded by a skillful articulation of the dilemma by the playwright, and a sobering naturalism in the delineation of character. It is this play that eventually fulfills Professor Shelley's demand for a New Zealand social drama, and it achieves these requirements not in a farmhouse setting, but in the dingy hotel bedroom of a Wellington prostitute.

A more complex and ambitious play on similar themes followed almost immediately: "The Evening Paper" has been considerably expanded and revised for its stage, radio, and television productions since its Unity Theatre premiere in 1953, but all versions deal with the self-perpetuating complacency of New Zealand family life, with an oppressive resolution as in "The Bonds of Love," but this time placed in a suburban context which made self-recognition almost obligatory for audiences. The original one-act version pivoted on a highly topical reference to the conquest of Everest by the New Zealand beekeeper Edmund Hillary on the eve of the coronation of Elizabeth II. However, this acme of national pride was applied ambivalently, finally becoming an impossible ideal for a family hopelessly committed to an unimaginatively patterned existence. Substantially before the arrival of Harold Pinter or Samuel Beckett, it was highly disconcerting for audiences to encounter a playwright arguing the inevitability of routine as the basis of behavior, the garrulous suburban matriarch as the engineer of relationships, and the newspaper as the only imaginative escape from domestic reality.

In Mason's last major Unity play, "The Verdict" (1955), the characters are bourgeois, the setting is a bar, and the topicality is intensified: the play was based on a much-publicized recent murder trial. Amid golfing chat, two married couples holidaying together discuss the verdict on an adolescent girl who murdered her father and thus exposed several family scandals. A woman in the bar, who is recognized as the girl's mother, demands the opportunity to speak in her own defense; her contention that the world is full of violence is supported by the exposure of the various vacationers as their sympathy generates a confessional mood. A moral parity is thus established among the characters through gestures of compromise and accommodation, and the play's conclusion is markedly optimistic beside its predecessors: by their adaptability, these characters prove their ability to weld together a new society that has abandoned its puritanical complacencies.

II *The Full-length Plays of the Late 1950s*

Mason wrote numerous other short plays and sketches for amateur production in the 1950s, but by 1956 his style and structural inclinations were already showing the constrictions of Unity production. "The Verdict" reflects a tendency toward more elaborately patterned dramatic construction, and its greater character range suggests a drift toward a larger, more public stage. Both of these developments culminate in three major full-length works in radically different modes written between 1956 and 1959.

The Pohutukawa Tree (1956), the first of Mason's works on Maori themes, developed from some real events that Mason had observed while managing a Tauranga orchard in 1952.[2] But the shift to Maori material also admitted a liberation of style; the severities of naturalism had become increasingly unacceptable to a writer with an impulse toward formal balance and metaphorical embellishment, both of which found ample latitude within the Maori tribal ethos. New Zealand's Maori population largely resisted the social restrictions of colonial puritanism, so that a play focussing on Maori characters easily avoids the problems of character convergence which result in the somewhat contrived social grouping in plays like "The Verdict." Aroha Mataira, the widowed protagonist of *The Pohutukawa Tree,* is clearly an atypical Maori, sharply differentiated from her relatives by her uncompromising adherence to an austere Protestantism which is patently untenable within the tribal context. In her character are embedded the ambiguities of "The Bonds of Love": the cohesive warmth of tribal philanthropy is subdued—but not extinguished—by the unequivocal demands of her essentially Old Testament God, so that when her son vandalizes a church and her daughter is seduced by a barman her immediate impulse is to reject them. However, it is here that the secondary European characters become important, effecting the beginnings of a cultural synthesis that brings a tone of optimism to the assertiveness of Aroha's ending. Aroha needs to be humanized, but the Anglican clergyman equally needs to be tribalized, as he acknowledges after visiting the *marae:* "there's such life there, such joy in simple things, so much music and laughter; such a wonderful distaste for those nagging things so important to us: time, security, money. I tell you, I found more true religion there, more real simplicity of spirit, than anywhere I've been here . . ."[3]

Critical discussion of *The Pohutukawa Tree,* as with Mason's later Maori plays, was largely concerned with social generalizations which were of little relevance to dramatic character creation. What is more important is the atmospheric power of the play in the theater, evidenced by more than sixty productions, testifying that Mason was the first dramatist to pass beyond the crude tourist perspective of the biracial basis of New Zealand society. The terms of Mason's advance are not strictly realistic; they involve a search for a national poetic self-expression through the fusion of familiar Maori rhetoric and symbolism with the stolid pragmatism of the Protestants, parodied in this case through the figure of Aroha Mataira. *Aroha,* the Maori word for "love," is the most prominent quality lacking in Mrs. Mataira's attenuated Christianity.

The Pohutukawa Tree was written specifically for production by the New Zealand Players, a professional company which between 1953 and 1960 toured lavish productions throughout the country; confidence in professional acting resources is reflected in the ambitious stylistic resonances of the play's longer speeches. A new stylistic flourish is also apparent in Mason's first full-length domestic play, "Birds in the Wilderness," written immediately after *The Pohutukawa Tree* and produced in Wellington and London in 1958. European cliché gives the play its title and sets the mood for a parodic comedy on the theme of national consolidation. Eight characters converge on a city house in response to a newspaper advertisement and decide to embark on a small-scale furniture-manufacturing industry, for which enterprise they have great enthusiasm but no basic skills. Two of the characters are Hungarians, a topical factor at the time of its writing, as Hungarian refugees arrived in New Zealand with little preparation. The action satirizes the notion of stabilizing a cosmopolitan society of aspirant "do-it-yourselfers" through a naive approach to industrialization, a theme still relevant to the essentially agricultural New Zealand economy after more than twenty years. The play effectively combines satire, comedy, and farce, and a professional revival directed by Mason himself in 1968 was a popular success.

The initial productions of *The Pohutukawa Tree* and "Birds in the Wilderness" had caused considerable organizational effort for Mason at a time when his own artistic energies were at peak. In 1958 he saw Emlyn Williams perform his one-man stage biographies of Dylan Thomas and Charles Dickens; he immediately thought of adapting the genre to accommodate New Zealand material, and, although Williams was scarcely encouraging, Mason began to construct a solo work for his own performance. Mason's acting experience extended back to the early years of Unity Theatre, and his voice had developed a professional versatility largely through radio performance; he had achieved prominence as a writer of short stories before he seriously turned to drama, and it was to this material that he first looked for sources of a solo work. "Summer's End," a long short story published in 1949, was redrafted and added to excerpts from some loosely autobiographical radio talks delivered about three years later, and the new work was entitled *The End of the Golden Weather: A Voyage into a New Zealand Childhood.* The origin of the title is acknowledged in the epigraph from Thomas Wolfe's *The Web and the Rock:* "The subject he chose for his first effort was a boy's vision of life over a ten-month period between his twelfth and thirteenth year, and the title was *The End of the Golden Weather.* By this title, he meant to describe that change in the *colour* of life which every child has known—the change from the enchanted light and weather of his soul, the full golden light, the magic green and gold in which he sees the earth in childhood. He prepared to tell how, at this period in a child's life, this strange and magic light—this *golden weather*—begins to change and, for the first time, some of the troubling weathers of a man's soul are revealed to him. . . ."[4]

Mason's short story had dealt with a ten-year-old boy, which meant that a continuous ambivalence arose when it was performed by a solo adult actor on a bare stage. After the initial tour Mason extensively revised *The End of the Golden Weather,* changing the narrative perspective and bringing the protagonist's age to accord with that suggested in the Wolfe epigraph; this accentuated the theme of mutability and the sense of the precarious fragility of the childhood vision, with the fictive protagonist torn between the adulthood of the actor and the receding childhood of his own fantasies. As in *The Pohutukawa Tree,* the fundamental dramatic tension comes from the impossible equipoise between past and future, but, more than any of Mason's other work, *The End of the Golden Weather* is concerned with diachronic process, an irrepressible evolutionary action.

"Sunday at Te Parenga," the first section of *The End of the Golden Weather,* sets the narrative in a seaside township in the north of New Zealand. The fluid presentational style means that the actor moves briefly into numerous secondary characters, so that the stage is soon populated by the local citizenry, including the narrator's family, his neighbors, the Reverend Thirle, Police Sergeant Robinson, and Firpo, a likable imbecile who identifies with the great athlete. In "The Night of the Riots," the Depression commotions reach Te Parenga, and the narrator watches unseen as the mounted policeman deals with local insurgents. This initiation into adult realism explicitly marks the end of childhood's "golden weather": "Ahead, the multi-coloured adult world, Man's Own Country, studded with grim effigies marked Greed, Authority, Pride and Law—armour to be assumed for adult occasions. And humour: kindness: sacred and redeeming graces as I had seen them and loved them in the old policeman—how easily, how willingly extinguished!"[5] These principles are realized dramatically in the second part of *The End of the Golden Weather*, "The Made Man," and remain in ominous suspension through the final section of the first part: "Christmas at Te Parenga" is essentially a comedy of Christmas festivities, effectively curtailed by a sobering awareness of the emotional complexities behind the occasion. "The Made Man" is considerably longer than the other sections, and again has a pattern of commitment and disillusionment: the narrator invests his ambitions in Firpo, a grotesque parody of adulthood, and watches as his imagined athletic prowess is ridiculed on the beach. By the end, the "armour" of adulthood has become an inevitability.

The End of the Golden Weather is effective drama only in performance, and the "reading text" contains no acting directions; to approach it as prose fiction is to miss its central purpose. The script is a record of performance, not a guide to performance, so that its essential value is to those who already know the work from the stage. Literary analysis of the script has thus sometimes focused on verbal detail which is sharply qualified by the expressivity of performance; the subtlety of Mason's acting means that gesture is rarely used simply to reinforce or illustrate a statement, but more usually to extend a contrapuntal development which may at times amount to self-parody. Between 1959 and 1978, when a serious operation interrupted an American appearance, Mason performed his solo work more than eight hundred and fifty times, including seasons in Britain, Australia, and the United States. A film version is radically different in style, reverting to a large, fully individualized cast; no solo actor has attempted to emulate Mason's stage virtuosity in the whole piece.

III   *The Maori Plays and Solo Works of the 1960s*

In the early 1960s Mason was largely occupied with intensive touring of *The End of the Golden Weather*, but he also profited from the improved facilities of the New Zealand Broadcasting Service by perfecting his radio technique, notably with an adaptation of "The Evening Paper" first broadcast in 1963. New Zealand professional theater was in decline after the collapse of the New Zealand Players, but a valuable production opportunity emerged with the foundation of the Downstage restaurant theater in Wellington in 1964, the first of the community theaters which are now prominent in most cities. However, in its initial stage Downstage Theatre operated on a minimal budget in an extremely constricting location, a converted coffee bar; its first production there was Edward Albee's *The Zoo Story*, directed by Owen Leeming and performed by Peter Bland and Martyn Sanderson (all three playwrights). Mason at that time was occupied with large-cast plays on Maori subjects, specifically for radio production.

Just as Mason's solo works assume the interpretative resources of his own performance, so are his four later Maori plays constructed around the unique vocal qualities of the great Maori bass Inia te Wiata. Te Wiata had first achieved international distinction at Covent Garden, where he sang numerous leading operatic roles in the 1950s, including two parts written for him by Benjamin Britten. He had diversified into films and musicals, achieving his most famous role in *The Most Happy Fella*, and in 1965 toured New Zealand in *Porgy and Bess*. The New Zealand Broadcasting Corporation was concerned to make the most of his visit to his homeland, and, among other ventures, commissioned a new play on a Maori theme from Mason, who responded by, eventually, writing four such radio plays for the voice of te Wiata.

Awatea was completed late in 1964 and was produced in 1965; it ran for over one hundred minutes, and is Mason's longest radio play. For te Wiata, Mason created the role of Werihe Paku, a blind Maori elder living on a clifftop in the North Island; Werihe's ambitions are invested in his son Matiu, whom he believes to be practicing medicine in Auckland, and the son's social status intensifies further the father's local standing at Omoana, "the place of the ocean." It emerges that the son failed medical school and has since been a freezing worker, but attempts to keep the truth from the old man are finally unsuccessful, and the play ends with Werihe ennobled by acceptance of the situation. The European characters are of little final importance to Werihe; apart from Gilhooly, the local postmistress on whom he depends for contact with his son, the Europeans are mainly instrumental in sustaining the deception, and their function is more closely related to the play's mechanics than to its theme. But in old Werihe's Maori context Mason created the most intense atmosphere of Maori community life in any of his plays: there are fourteen named Maori parts and a similar number of supernumeraries, several of the climactic speeches are in Maori, the second act involves the annual

festival of the *hui,* and the resolution presents a slight relaxation of
the Maori ethos to accommodate a European principle. For the play's
second edition in 1978, Mason deleted the original introduction in
which he described the play's factual sources and his research
methods, and introduced a second appendix consisting of letters
written by Matiu to his father. This increases the nonfictional resonance of the play, it elaborates the character of Matiu (giving him
social—if not dramatic—parity with his father), and it makes the play
more overtly a community drama, concerned with the fundamental
cohesion of a rapidly evolving society.

Mason's researching for *Awatea* produced an abundance of material: "My imagination was occupied for a time by an old Maori father,
devoted to the old ways and imperatives, searching for his wild son,
who had lost them in the city; sometimes I saw a bardic Maori
bursting joyously through the narrow straits of pakeha feelings and
emotions, finding his true image and stature only in death."[6] "The
Hand on the Rail" and "Swan Song," the two Maori radio plays
written immediately after *Awatea,* explore similar situations. "The
Hand on the Rail" again involves a rural Maori elder trying to make
contact with his son who has disappeared into a corrupting urban
environment; a policeman, identical in name with a character in
Awatea, assists the old man in tracing his son through a sordid
Auckland setting. Though this is a relatively slight play in terms of
social portraiture, it is more cohesive structurally than *Awatea* because its central quest motif means that the old man's enlightenment
may be protracted through most of the action. The heavy dramatic
ironies that give *Awatea* much of its bold impact are here replaced by
subtleties and implications as the audience, with the old man, slowly
untangles his son's career and the consequences of his rebellion
against Maori values. The son's suicide leaves the old man to return
home to his European wife at the end of the play, bringing his infant
grandson, in whose upbringing will be tested the principles of cultural convergence that the old man has observed. "The Hand on the
Rail" is a more explicit study of the factors behind fragmentation and
integration than *The Pohutukawa Tree* or *Awatea;* for the first time,
Mason's Maori elder is married, and the biracial source of the com-
plications is documented in enough detail to admit the hope of future
remedy.

In "Swan Song" the protagonist is again a Maori elder, and his
commitment to Italian opera emphasizes the influence of Inia te
Wiata as the prospective performer of the lead role. The play's action
involves old Smithson, dying of leukemia, being taken by his part-

Maori daughter Kura on a final tour of New Zealand; bad weather isolates them in Milford Sound with other tourists, among whom is an opera singer, and the play dissolves into an expressionistic death scene in which operatic motifs become formally dynamic. "Swan Song" has a particular interest among Mason's Maori plays because of its portrayal of old Smithson. In *The Pohutukawa Tree* and *Awatea* the Maori elder is a powerful, monolithic repository of authority; in "The Hand on the Rail" he shows himself ready to adapt, but in "Swan Song" he is himself the rebel, rejecting fixed values which are here invested in his puritanical daughter. Finally, Smithson does not need a family, a community, or a social position; his unpretentious eclecticism freely accommodates diverse elements, giving his final scene a serenity that is unusual among Mason's Maori characters.

Having quadrupled his Maori works within six months, Mason now turned his writing energies toward Downstage Theatre, of which he had become vice president. In May 1965, Downstage looked back on a high level of artistic enterprise and box office success, but also on economic pressures that made the viability of a seventy-five seat restaurant theater dubious. To save the theater from imminent collapse, Mason volunteered to write and perform a new solo work; the result was "To Russia, with Love," written and learned in a week, and based on a visit to the U.S.S.R. in 1958.

"To Russia, with Love" is set in Moscow, and has three central characters. At the start the actor is dressed in a gaudy Mexican poncho, a gray goatskin Russian hat, and his black working rig underneath; he is in the character of Eugene B. Timms of Castroville, Texas, dictating a taped message to his wife from his room in the Metropol Hotel. The episode consists mainly of comic caricature, but it also introduces more serious elements, particularly the figure of Irving Davis, a young Californian law graduate who is hawking old copies of *Time* to help finance his travels. With a change of coat, the actor becomes Davis, greeting Timms as he leaves with his interpreter for his token visit to the Bolshoi Ballet. Davis is approached by Dmitri, a young Russian aged twenty-four, who warns him about selling Western literature and covertly invites him to his flat for the evening; attracted by the idea, Davis telephones his embassy, and then defiantly calls a taxi. For the last section, the actor wears a Russian tunic and boots and becomes Dmitri, entertaining Davis in his flat. Speaking as "the tiny voice of the Loyal Opposition,"[7] Dmitri articulates the problems facing a sensitive young intellectual in the U.S.S.R., and tries to persuade Davis to smuggle out a contribution to Amnesty International's *Chronicle of Current Events*. Davis's reluctance does not undermine their mutual respect, but the conclusion of the piece involves the reaffirmation of the reality of the Cold War, strikingly opposed to the atmosphere of cultural or spiritual integration that typifies the resolution of most of Mason's works.

Several important details in "To Russia, with Love" were extremely topical at the time of its first production, and this necessitated updating when its first tour was completed. The two other works that have served as companion pieces to complement the program are also factual in origin, but sufficiently distanced in time to retain a period impact. For his first performances outside Wellington, Mason placed an interval after the Dmitri/Davis encounter, and then performed "The Last Supper," a grim study of an American family disintegrating after being contaminated by radioactive particles; even the names were retained from the original disaster in Texas in 1957, and the combined program, entitled "The Counsels of the Wood," thus framed its Moscow episodes neatly within the Texan perspective. Mason's view was that "The piece sought to demonstrate a Camusian view of limits: that we have gone too far in unspiritualised technology and that, for the future of the race, we must call a halt."[8] "The Last Supper" was eventually deleted from the program because "the creative technology preached by R. Buckminster Fuller seemed to make it obsolete,"[9] and it was replaced by "The Waters of Silence." In the 1970s "To Russia, with Love" was preceded by "The Waters of Silence," and the whole program entitled "Men of Soul."

In 1965 "The Waters of Silence" was conceived and always performed as a discrete work, with the French and English versions forming complementary halves of a single program; Downstage Theatre organized extensive school touring in 1966. Though "The Waters of Silence" was also written at great speed (in a fortnight, for another Downstage emergency), the source was at least literary: Vercors's famous document of the French resistance, *Le Silence de la mer*. In the first week Mason adapted Vercors into an English stage version for solo actor, and in the second week he translated his adaptation back into French and learned it. Adaptation involved a radical change of perspective: whereas *Le Silence de la mer* is written from the point of view of the Frenchman who is forced to billet the German officer Ebrennac, the actor in "The Waters of Silence" plays Ebrennac himself, surrounded by a Coventry-like silence. Ebrennac is naive enough to believe that war will bring valuable cultural and spiritual byproducts, and his disillusionment parallels that of the central character in *The End of the Golden Weather;* as with "To Russia, with Love," there can be no convergence at the end of "The

Waters of Silence," merely an awareness of incompatibility.

Considerable technical variation may be observed among Mason's early solo works. In *The End of the Golden Weather* the performer/narrator moves in and out of about forty characters, and visual narrative often generates irony against the spoken: a gesture of the performer often overtly parodies the words of the character. In "To Russia, with Love" the basic structure consists of three extended monologues to an implied on-stage audience, so that the actor stays in character for a substantial period, with word and gesture usually relating sympathetically. But in "The Waters of Silence" the isolation of the actor reflects logically the historical seclusion of the character, so that in the barrier of silence reality and theatricality become inseparable.

With three substantial solo works, Mason was again occupied with extensive touring until the prospect of another visit by Inia te Wiata in 1968 directed him again to Maori themes. This time, te Wiata was primarily concerned with the stage premiere of *Awatea,* presented by Downstage Theatre in the Wellington Town Hall. Commercially, the production was extremely successful, but artistic inadequacies were inevitable in using a huge civic building for a play constructed in intimate human terms rather than spectacular pageantry.

As *Awatea* entered rehearsal, Mason was completing another radio play on a historical Maori theme: that of Hongi Hika who, taken to England as a specimen of a noble savage, addressed George IV as "Mister King George." The radio commission was for a short play using only one Maori character, and this Mason achieved by focusing on Hongi in an official context in Britain, and from a missionary perspective in New Zealand. As in *The Pohutukawa Tree,* the Maori protagonist's perception of flaws in the Christian context results in a reversion to the primitive, although the savagery of Hongi's regression finds no parallel in Aroha Mataira. By the end of the play, the missionaries, like their king, are thoroughly compromised. They have acquired protection by condoning Hongi's tribal atrocities, and they remain helpless observers as cannibalistic grotesqueries increase; the play ends with a wry ambivalence as the missionary attempts to intone a Christian ceremony over Hongi's deathbed, while the chief anticipates a pagan afterlife. Mason's use of Maori names and titles often conceals an irony: "Awatea" means "light," and "Hongi" refers to a Maori form of greeting, by rubbing noses. Of all the plays on Maori themes, *Hongi* most emphatically denies cultural synthesis at the end.

IV   *Bruce Mason in the 1970s*

With *Hongi* Mason completed his cycle of plays on Maori themes, and the emergence of young Maori writers in the 1960s had aroused the hope—unfulfilled in the 1970s—that the full-length Maori plays of the future would no longer be the work of European writers. Though critical evaluations of Mason's Maori plays have varied widely, there can be no question that he carried the genre far beyond the achievement of Leitch's "The Land of the Moa" (1895), Douglas Stewart's *The Golden Lover* (1944), or James Ritchie's works of the 1960s, produced on both radio and stage. The only other dramatic work on a Maori subject to draw substantial critical attention in the 1960s was Jenny McLeod's multimedia treatment of Maori mythology, "Earth and Sky" (1968), the analysis of which must be primarily musical.

In the late 1960s Mason became deeply interested in the movements and ideologies of the radical young, and dramatized some of the tensions of the generation gap in *Zero Inn* (1970). A hippy rock group, following the principles of *I Ching*, arrives at the lakeside vacation cabin of an incontrovertibly bourgeois middle-aged man, staying with his wife and mother-in-law. The Christmas context aggravates their disagreement about materialistic and puritanical issues, and several characters tentatively cross the generation gap; eventually, the businessman calls the police because the hippies are carrying cannabis. *Zero Inn* thus belongs very much to the late 1960s, when counter-cultural movements accentuated the polarization of the rebellious young and their conservative elders, and in subsequent reworkings of this material Mason stylized the play's mechanics by introducing tape-recorded effects and photographic slides, with a Brechtian controller of the action. In an even later treatment, entitled "The Need to Fail," the conclusion is invested with overt didacticism, so that defamiliarization replaces the psychological characterization of the original play.

A widening of stylistic possibilities may also be observed in Mason's stage adaptations of his Maori radio plays, work which occupied him at about the period of his *Zero Inn* revisions. In each case, the expansive radio material is substantially reshaped, demanding an inventive approach to stagecraft to which the New Zealand theater has been remarkably slow to respond. The original *Zero Inn* has inevitably become a period piece, and as such may well achieve its greatest popularity; this has happened with "Suitcases," a double bill for a single cast, consisting of "The Evening Paper" and "Virtuous Circle" (formerly "The Light Enlarging"), a situational comedy on an operatic theme.

In 1973 Mason returned to his solo works, and the demand for performances of *The End of the Golden Weather* and "Men of Soul" continued until ill health interrupted his acting in 1978. In 1976 he premiered two new solo works, "Not Christmas, but Guy Fawkes" and "Courting Blackbird," and subsequently retained all four works in repertoire, although "Men of Soul" was performed less frequently.

"Not Christmas, but Guy Fawkes" was commissioned by the New Zealand Ministry of Foreign Affairs and the Queen Elizabeth II Arts Council for performance at the South Pacific Festival of Arts at Rotorua in March 1976. The work consists of four sections which were rearranged during its first year, during which time the opening piece, "The Glass Wig" (based on a 1947 short story),[10] was replaced by "Narcissus Observed," an autobiographical work based on Mason's "Beginnings."[11] From the world of Te Parenga, now viewed from the distance of manhood, the young Narcissus moves through adolescence until his university studies are interrupted—momentarily—by a voice on the radio announcing the outbreak of war. "Et in Arcadia Ego: A Snobs' Pageant," also derived from a *Landfall* autobiographical piece,[12] finds the "raw, country lad," uniformed, at London's Churchill Club for servicemen; his youthful artistic proclivities are here indulged by mixing with T.S. Eliot, E.M. Forster, Stephen Spender, Henry Moore, and the Sitwells, but an ironical tone dominates the piece as the narrator views the naiveté of his younger self. The third section, "Limp Bananas: An Occult Farce," had its origin as a radio piece and presents Narcissus as pianist and music critic in Wellington about fifteen years after the war. The satirical comedy of the pretentious musical world is highly engaging, with taped piano music frequently used for parody, but the many allusions to Luigi Bonpensière's *New Pathways to Piano Technique* are imperfectly integrated into the central narrative, with the "occult" keyboard methodology being introduced late, considering its importance to the satirical resolution.

"The Conch Shell," which makes up the second half of "Not Christmas, but Guy Fawkes," originated as a short story first published in 1958,[13] which Mason adapted as an (unproduced) television play in about 1968, refining it to its solo form in 1976. All versions are set at Te Parenga and involve a relationship between Ginger Finucane, an ugly eleven-year-old Irish boy, and the narrator, his classmate, from a much better family. Bullying eventually reduces

Ginger to a state of desperation, and, in a scene of bizarre comedy, he takes advantage of the narrator's boyish ethics to blackmail him into a situation in which he must sacrifice half his books, half his shell collection, even half of his pocket money; these are mostly returned as the boys reach adolescence and grow out of the emotions and ethics that governed their bullying and blackmail. In a coda, set in London in about 1950, the narrator visits the Embassy Theatre to find, astonishingly, Ginger Finucane playing the Clown in *Love's Labours Lost;* backstage afterwards, Ginger only vaguely remembers the narrator and has little idea where he acquired the conch shell which he keeps for luck. Though the earlier sections of "Not Christmas, but Guy Fawkes" are rich in satire and self-deflation, "The Conch Shell" exceeds them in scope, achieving in its sympathetic study of "the butt of the class" the fragile perspective of childhood that dominates *The End of the Golden Weather.*

"Courting Blackbird" has no apparent antecedent within Mason's writings, and it is the most clearly unified of his full-length solo programs, a single, cohesive chronological sweep taking in the whole biographical narrative. The authorial raconteur presides over the episodic life story of Boris (Bo) Godunov Baron, in whose highly idiosyncratic career he was intermittently involved. Subtitled "A theme and variations in the baroque style," "Courting Blackbird" establishes its leading theme in the opening section: an eccentric Jewish couple in London deciding to export their intractable only son to Wellington on the eve of World War II. The six variations and coda which follow present "Bo Baron and the Impressionable Young" (Bo's ascendancy over the narrator), "Bo Baron and the Bourgeoisie" (Bo attempts to convert his aunt and uncle to Marxism), "Bo Baron, Love and Marriage" (Bo marries a unionist's daughter, which cures him of proletarian sympathies), "Bo Baron and Higher Education" (Bo's rise and fall as a student hero), "Bo Baron and the War for Civilisation" (Bo disappears while serving in Egypt), "Bo Baron and the Ineffable Light" (Bo, released from a Soviet camp in 1951, dies without regaining his sanity), and the Coda, in which the narrator explains the title allusion.

In his portrait of his younger self as a malleable searcher for a heroic model, the narrator relates to Bo as, earlier, he did to Firpo. But the pattern of disillusionment differs; Firpo is instantly recognizable as a false idol, but Bo's downfall, though predictable in general terms, is effected by the extraneous instrumentation of a Stalinist concentration camp. This means that there is no pervasive irony, so that Bo's death is a shock which by contrast intensifies the value placed on his earlier vitality. Totalitarian oppression is even more ruthless in its levelling than in "To Russia, with Love," but the vicious truncation of Bo's career is not only acceptable but dramaturgically obligatory in terms of the expressionistic development of the work. Like Strindberg in his "chamber plays," Mason fuses musical form with subjective, self-determining narration; from a single premise (Bo comes to New Zealand), the controlling consciousness uses a stream of associative linking to move through a cumulative series of confrontations between the protagonist and the social environment into which he is propelled. For Strindberg, the only way to terminate such an action is by waking from the hallucination, by making contact again with the severity of external reality. This Mason achieves by invoking Stalinism, the antithesis of the impulse toward cultural reconstruction which activates many of his characters, martyrs as well as clowns.

CHAPTER 5

The Plays of James K. Baxter

THE importance of James K. Baxter to the development of New Zealand drama is remarkable, considering that his sense of theatrical strategy remained crude throughout his career and that none of his twenty-four extant plays received the meticulous revision that was invested in most of his poetry. Playwriting was to Baxter largely a recreational activity, and the sporadic nature of his dramatic output was governed largely by the enthusiasm of local directors. However, the diversity of Baxter's literary skills was such that even patently flawed plays are often noteworthy for the novelty of their terms of failure and for their articulation of particular dramatic problems. Even a light commercial success like Roger Hall's *Glide Time* (1976) follows the—partly negative—example of Baxter's work a decade earlier.

I *The Radio Plays*

Sophisticated production of radio drama in New Zealand became possible with the establishment of new studios in the late 1950s, and the advisory services of the New Zealand Broadcasting Service enabled many writers to diversify their work. Baxter, however, was somewhat in advance of this transition, and dealing with his first script was a substantial educational exercise for the production team: *Jack Winter's Dream* was accepted in May 1956 and finally produced in August 1958, with a stage version following in 1960 and a feature film treatment in 1979.

The primary source of Baxter's material lay in conversations with his father about the Naseby goldfields, and he acknowledged the dramaturgic influence of Dylan Thomas's *Under Milk Wood* and Laurie Lee's *Magellan;* [1] to these he might have added Josef and Karel Capek's *The Life of the Insects* and the poetry of Alistair Campbell. The central story, which may be attributed to Baxter's father and which makes up Winter's dream, is a simple goldfields melodrama involving seduction, robbery, and murder; but, before the action

reaches melodramatic resolution, the dream fades out into an objective morning scene and the discovery of the dreamer's dead body.
The dream is framed by a scene of Jack Winter drinking by himself at
the start, with the hallucinatory catalyst objectified as the female
"Bottle," and by the brief final episode in which two girl hikers find
his corpse; a Narrator appears frequently throughout, even during
the dream. By this device the dream sequence is continually related
to Winter's presence, and the imagery is used extensively to suggest
that the dream environment is an animistic projection of Winter's
identity.

Baxter's central theme, recurrent through all his work, is mutability, the process by which the old alcoholic's body is accommodated
into the earth again; the insistent imagery of "clay," extending even to
the sun-dried mud hut where Winter dies, is a continuous reminder
of the frailty of men. Women, by contrast, are constructed of "rock,"
immune or insensitive to the forces of carnal decay; Bottle has a
female voice, and the hikers simply find the clay quaint. The dream
population is a predatory ghost world, quasi-historical figures haunting Winter's refuge, resurrected from their graves to meet the dying
man halfway. In *Jack Winter's Dream* a playwright had at last followed
up the expressionistic method pioneered in New Zealand by Eric
Bradwell, and, by a curious coincidence, he did it partly by an
animistic projection of "clay" imagery.

Ten years, and several stage plays, separate *Jack Winter's Dream*
from Baxter's next radio play, "The First Wife" (1966), but the techniques are remarkably similar. Instead of the old drunkard's perspective, Baxter used a vision that is easily recognizable as his own, and
the action is implicitly located at Brighton beach, twelve miles south
of Dunedin, where he himself grew up; instead of populating the
vision with the ghosts of miners, he used what he saw as fragments of
his own identity, some of which he had used before in poems and
prose works. The play begins objectively with a family on vacation at
the beach. The wife rejects the Man's embraces, and he retreats into a
nostalgic reverie in which he meets, on the beach, his Younger Self, a
Sea Woman (Lilith, the archetypal "other woman"), and his Ancestor,
who reminds him of his responsibility in marriage so that the vision
can fade out into an objective scene of marital reconciliation. The final
tone of didacticism is crude, and the rejection of Lilith also implies
rejection of the animistic, Edenic Brighton, an attitude which remains unconvincing. But the main flaw concerns the function and
definition of the speaking parts; Baxter allows himself too few "secret
selves" to convey any emotional or moral complexity, and defines

them with self-conscious precision. The stark under-population of "The First Wife" makes it among Baxter's least successful plays, but it does reflect a move toward a subjective dramaturgy, where his greatest strength lay.

Baxter never again confronted personal archetypes directly in his plays. In his other two radio plays of the same period confrontation is oblique, softened by a myth that is summarized at the start: "Mr. Brandywine Chooses a Gravestone" is a development of the Old Testament story of Daniel, and "Who Killed Sebastian" begins with a narrative of the martyrdom. In an introductory note Baxter explains that Daniel Brandywine is a modern Catholic Everyman, an unenterprising bourgeois stereotype faced with death, and the play's action consists of a renewal of contact with his own inner self. A brief biblical passage establishes the prototype. Then Daniel moves from his doctor's rooms to a confessional and from there to his pub; having received no real satisfaction from doctor, priest, or barman, Daniel at last confronts his menopausal wife, Moira, but they go to bed without his breaking the news that he has only a few months to live. In Daniel's dream a Doppelgänger technique is introduced, ostensibly new characters speaking with the voices of established characters. In part, this suggests that Daniel is interpreting new situations in the only terms that make sense to him, but it also implies a deepening contact with his inner self. A barman/guardian allows Daniel to pass through a stone wall, where he meets his mother in a surrealistic context; his father appears, and then Daniel encounters a priest/stonemason who explains a little about the schizoid identity that is reflected in the labyrinth of caves that Daniel moves through. Dulcie, a Lilith-type figure whom Daniel left twenty years ago, appears, and he acknowledges his inability to love anybody; his wife wakes him from his dream, he tells her of his illness, and the play ends with a reassertion of marital harmony.

In spite of its weak ending, "Mr. Brandywine Chooses a Gravestone" is one of Baxter's most complex and coherent plays. The dream and the biblical archetype serve as complementary catalysts to the hallucinatory narrative, and the collocation of stable and unstable identities within the secondary characterization effectively dramatizes Daniel's search for his essential self, as it is to find expression on his gravestone.

"Who Killed Sebastian," Baxter's last radio play to be produced, was written in 1967, when he was thinking primarily in stage terms. The martyrdom story serves as a preface to a domestic situation in which a middle-aged bourgeois couple argues with friends and relatives about responsibility for their son's death in a motorcycle accident; drugs, homosexuality, the motorcycle, and an Oedipus complex are the ostensible background, but attention becomes fixed on the mindless materialism of the parents. The stereotyped nature of the material is compounded by the persistence throughout of a didactic tone which intrudes only toward the end of Baxter's two previous radio plays.

The theme is explored more cogently in a stage play of the same period, "Requiem for Sebastian," a verse dialogue for three voices; less social detail contributes to much greater fluidity in this version, but, inexplicably, the stage play does not overtly capitalize on the dramatic potential of the martyrdom. Related in content is "The Hero," a short stage play written in the same year; technically, it contains expressionistic elements which make it distinct from Baxter's other stage plays. A stereotyped man and wife talk about their son who died in Vietnam; the son enters, in a bloodstained uniform, and relates the truth about the war, though throughout the play his parents neither see nor hear him. Allocation of blame becomes more complex than in the Sebastian plays for the son is as ignorantly committed to the Vietnam situation as anyone else; his posture offers neither an indictment nor a vindication of heroism.

II The Alcoholic Subculture on Stage

Whereas radio drama is an art form existing in time but not in space, not far removed from the art of the poet who employs personae, the theater requires that each voice be related to a spatial dimension. In his radio plays Baxter could carry his voices freely through time without having to worry about other behavioral encumbrances; flesh could mingle with clay, the future with the ancestral past, with the opportunity of limiting confrontation to a purely auditory level. But for the stage greater expressive resources also meant greater constrictions; the spatial presence of the flesh also required its spatial consistency, and the consequences of verbal behavior had to be plotted in physical terms.

The large numbers of alcoholics in Baxter's stage plays may be partly explained by the fact that the first of these, *The Wide Open Cage* (1959), was written just after he himself had stopped drinking; his alcoholic experience had left him with a wealth of anecdote which seemed dramatically useful, and a lot of painful memories which he attempted to exorcise in the theater. Also, he had so long been accustomed to people laughing at his own drunken clowning that it was easy for him to attempt to transfer it onto the stage. But selecting characters from an alcoholic subculture also offered a solution to a major dramaturgic problem: with the use of alcohol to govern both vocal and physical behavior, Baxter managed to invest causation not only in the normal principles of character contact which determine the progression of social drama, but also in the whisky bottle which can liberate characters from the pattern of social decencies. Alcoholic characters provided Baxter with an opportunity for dramatized poetic utterance, for the virtual elimination of the subtleties of motivation, and for the reduction of a whole drama to an almost subhuman level of survival. Most of his drunks have a long career of alcoholism behind them, and have had either all vestiges of ambition knocked out of them, or have learned to limit their ambitions to easily accessible goals. They are mostly cornered men, ready to retreat into their shack, their pub, or their band rotunda the moment their dubious freedom is challenged; their capacity for aggression is limited to hysterical reactions or thoughtless betrayals.

These generalizations apply to most of Baxter's social plays, but they are firmly established in *The Wide Open Cage*. The setting is a shack in which lives Jack Skully, a nondrinking alcoholic in his fifties, and the cast consists of his visitors: his landlady, a youth, two girls, and Ben Hogan, Skully's former drinking companion, just released from jail and searching for his betrayer. Hogan and the priest both function as negative examples, offering alternative forms of bondage to Skully, but evasion of their influences leaves him in the paradoxical cage of the title: when one move outside the cage will put him in more desperate confinement than his present circumstances, it is better to enjoy the illusion of freedom that he finds inside his wide open cage.

The complication is both external and involuntary. Skully wins at the races but finds himself incapable of using the money without moving outside the cage; Hogan, who suspects him of having informed the police, murders him and takes the money. Similarly, the instrument of the catastrophe is involuntary and impersonal; the non-Christian revenge principle that dictates the ending comes when an ancient Maori skull belonging to Skully suddenly speaks, telling Hogan what to do. The skull is a complex symbol, signifying revenge, mutability, death, primitivism, and Golgotha, none of which is allowed a fixed value.

Orthodox Christianity is never allowed to triumph in Baxter's stage plays, and when *The Wide Open Cage* was produced off-Broadway in 1962 several critics compared the ambivalence of Baxter's treatment of Christian themes with that of Graham Greene. Baxter's stage plays characteristically invert biblical archetypes and employ religious role-playing with extreme contrasts between the characters and their metatheatrical roles. In *The Village Voice* Richard Sharp called the play a "contemporary passion play" and pointed out the clear analogies between the characters and Christ, Magdalene, Judas, and Christ's mother.[2] The rigidity of Sharp's equations, however, was wrong, because neither Skully nor Hogan may be completely identified with Christ or Judas. Baxter's characteristically schizoid role allocation involves two potential Christs meeting in a present-day Golgotha, with the loser eventually getting the role of Judas.

Although Baxter voiced scorn at the comments of Wellington critics, he was sufficiently moved by the observations of James Bertram and J.G.A. Pocock[3] about his language and characterization to attempt conventional realism in his next play, "Three Women and the Sea" (1961); this was a thorough failure, and left no doubt about Baxter's ineptitude at naturalistic dialogue. In 1962, he wrote "The Spots of the Leopard," a crude attempt at a more theatrical style which did not achieve production until 1967.

It was not until he became familiar with Dunedin's Globe Theatre in 1967 that Baxter returned to his alcoholic subculture for material for a new play. In several ways *The Band Rotunda* appears as an attempt to rework *The Wide Open Cage* in more blatant terms. The supply of alcoholics is more generous: the named characters are described as "A drunk," "A drunk," "An elderly drunk," "A young man," and "A drunk." Also, the religious role-playing is more heavily explicit: the "elderly drunk" actually recites the Twenty-second Psalm before his betrayal to the police, and Baxter's introduction names him as "the Christ of the play."[4] A New Zealand critic, Hal Smith, followed Richard Sharp in the critical identification of roles,[5] again extending the analysis too far; it is clear that although the old alcoholic is obsessed with the role of Christ, the identification is not accepted by any of the other characters. Two crosses are offered, and the old man chooses the black one; Grady, another drunk, appeals to a quite different Christ, a "dirty mad old" Christ.[6]

Baxter's drunks are a microcosm. Grady's Christ is dirty simply because Grady's whole world is dirty. In his introduction to the published script Baxter stated that "the material of the play was subconscious, personal and highly familiar, since I am myself a member of the great tribe of drunks who hold a mirror to the world of chaos we inhabit."[7] The conception of a colony of alcoholics as a mirror to the rest of the world is essentially the same as the expressionism of

Baxter's early radio plays; the most explicit parallel is Jack Winter's Bottle which precipitates a vision of the world. The dramaturgic problem lay in finding a method of containing the dramatized mirror vision so that the subjectivity of the mirror might be acknowledged without rendering the reflected chaos unrecognizable. In the radio plays this was easy: the character and situation of the dreamer could be established at the start, and the audience's response to the dream would be constantly governed by what it knew of the dreamer. On stage, it was not sufficient that the drunks should merely talk about the Christ they see in their mirror; the audience must be able to see the mirror, too. The most obvious solution, the Brechtian use of an authorial presence, was not acceptable to Baxter, possibly because of his abortive attempt to use the device in "The Spots of the Leopard." But in *The Band Rotunda* he discovered a technique of interfacing one kind of reality with another and, by a process of distorted reflection, forcing audiences into a position of revaluation. This happens most clearly in the antiphonal preaching of the "elderly drunk" and the Salvationist Captain, but in numerous places there is a tension between the utterance of a biblical text and the vehicle for that utterance.

The patterning of the play is largely determined by the fact that it happens on Good Friday. This establishes expectations in the audience which the resolution of the action generally fulfills. The characters are involuntarily caught up in a distorted reenactment of Good Friday, and the grossness of the distortion means that the audience is drawn not toward biblical illustration but toward the nature of the authorial mirror.

In a radio talk Baxter commented on Grady's controversial speech to his Christ: "My own Christian soul was by no means overjoyed by it; but when I write a play I am concerned not with edification but with dramatic truth expressed through a series of illusions. I am not Concrete Grady, though Concrete Grady is one of my secret selves."[8] For the characters in a play to represent an objectification of authorial "secret selves" is a central principle of Strindbergian expressionism, a principle with the potential of fusing the subjectivity of a private vision with the ostensible objectivity of a world of chaos in which biblical archetypes are mutilated. But though this is viable dramaturgic theory it was by no means fully realized in *The Band Rotunda*; there is nothing internal to identify the characters as a collection of the author's "secret selves," and so audiences would be left trying to locate the action within society or within biblical structures, without realizing that the whole microcosm was to be located within the playwright.

The complete vindication of this method did not come until the last of Baxter's plays dealing with New Testament material in an alcoholic context. "The Day that Flanagan Died" (1969). Again, biblical roles are heavily apparent; the characters who gather in Flanagan's pub after his death include his disciples, Matt, Peter (a fisherman), and John, his mother (named Mary), and a girl pregnant by him who is explicitly compared with Mary Magdalene. There is also a chorus of three old women who suggest Fates, a Policeman, a Doctor, a Professor, and the ubiquitous Priest; the last two contribute most of the religious commentary. Flanagan's resurrection in the penultimate scene is ostensibly precipitated by the Professor's pouring beer over his coffin; he explains his death and attempts to justify his life to his mother, who is sufficiently moved by his resurgence to pardon the pregnant girl. The play ends with the reassertion of domestic harmony in the pub, some comic irony in the Professor's confession of failure in his attempt to bring Flanagan back to life, and a reflective conversation between the girl and the Priest.

In its construction "The Day that Flanagan Died" is the most evenly successful of Baxter's stage plays. Again, there is a high degree of ambiguity between the social roles of his characters and their New Testament roles, but the terms of this ambiguity are defined with a precision that is found in no other play. The title establishes an authorial presidency that makes subjectivity inescapable; since the audience is led to expect a stage version of Baxter's best-known ballad,[9] this immediately suggests that the characters will approximate to the playwright's "secret selves." The early action suggests that the play is to be a simple expansion of the poem, but a complexity arises when Mary Flanagan and the Priest talk about the two crucified thieves, a motif later amplified by Flanagan himself: "There was good Flanagan and bad Flanagan, two horses in the same race. If one should win, half of me was gone . . . "[10] Baxter's familiar schizoid characterization is here expanded by allusion to the Descent into Hell and the text "Christ was made sin for us."[11] At the end of the play recitation of the ballad has the compelling effect of recapitulation and overt authorial synthesis; the narrative consciousness has fragmented itself into characters and parts of characters, and gradually coheres again, crystallizing into the ballad.

The characters in "The Day that Flanagan Died" are functions of the author, making explicit a tendency in all of Baxter's plays. The script is almost totally devoid of any subtextual dimension other than

New Testament allusion; the meaning of the dialogue is usually immediately apparent, and the characters seem to exist almost exclusively *for* that dialogue. There is no description of a set, stage directions are minimal, and each scene is introduced simply with the names of the characters. The only past that the characters have is the past that Flanagan and his pub have given them, and when their conversation becomes prospective it is generally concerned with following his example. Such mechanical starkness, extreme even for a Baxter play, accentuates the sense of authorial presidency.

Because Baxter in this play ignores subtleties of character creation, his individual characters have no real transfer value outside the play; they exist not for their individual value but holistically, as fractions of a more expansive value that constitutes the play. Baxter revealed the deliberateness of this technique in a radio talk, relating characterization to "the incurable pantheism of the human soul," and quoting H.D.F. Kitto's opinion that to Aristotle "plot" meant "mythos," "the arrangement of the total drama in the dramatist's mind, embodied in his script."[12] Such a rationalization neatly vindicates the limitations of Baxter's dramatic skills, and his best work developed from premises such as the dominance of the "dramatist's mind." Regrettably, he seldom found the courage to acknowledge this overtly in his technique.

III   *Mythic Revaluations on Stage*

As early as *The Wide Open Cage* Baxter had been exhorted to follow Greek precedent, and he argued—unconvincingly—that parallels might be drawn between "The Spots of the Leopard" and the Prometheus legend,[13] an opinion possibly supported by the director Richard Campion's description of it as "what pundits would call total theatre with borrowings from all well-known playwrights from Ionesco to Aeschylus."[14] But it seems more likely that the imposition of a mythic element was an example of Baxter's tendency toward retrospective schematization: by the time of the premiere of "The Spots of the Leopard," Baxter had already written "The Bureaucrat," another play derived from his experiences as a public servant in Wellington, explicitly based on Aeschylus's *Prometheus Bound*.

"The Bureaucrat" is set in an office in the School Publications Department of the Ministry of Education, Wellington. The play begins with a realistic episode in which the director, Fireman, lectures one of his staff, Harness, about punctuation; Fireman is obsessed with the missionary role of educationalists, and he offers an analogy which he develops into the myth of Prometheus. The awkwardness of the play begins with the length of time the characters take to discover what the audience has known from a glance at the program. Even without Baxter's program note explaining that Fireman "is a modern Prometheus chained to a desk instead of a rock,"[15] the characters' names make the Greek element obvious. When an office girl called Io enters and immediately starts explaining the significance of her name, the play descends to a level of banality from which it cannot recover. Richard Campion rightly observed that the Greek myth is "over-explicit and over-worked, alienating rather than enlightening," and Philip Smithells, also with some justice, praised Baxter's "faultless perception of New Zealand society, its endemic speech and language."[16] Professor Smithells's hyperbole has some basis, but the fundamental conflict of purpose between mythic resonance and satirical relevance was allowed to mar several of Baxter's later plays.

Baxter's own uncertainty about the best approach to classical myth in drama is indicated by the fact that, at almost the same time as he wrote "The Bureaucrat," he was also reworking the Philoctetes story within a Greek context, even though he saw it as illustrating a facet of modern life. In his introduction to The Sore-footed Man (1967) Baxter describes his Philoctetes as a "beat" type (explicitly using Norman Mailer's terminology) and his Odysseus as a "hip" type.[17] It seems likely that a crucial influence toward placing such types within a Greek context was Giraudoux's La Guerre de Troie n'aura pas lieu;[18] broadly, Baxter's method was to transpose Giraudoux's characters and themes into Sophocles's situation, as if La Guerre de Troie n'aura pas lieu were retold from the Greek angle, with a tone closer to urbane French comedy than to Greek tragedy. Like Giraudoux, Baxter used as his central theme the process of military commitment; Philoctetes replaces Hector as the peace-loving warrior who would rather be a nonentity than a hero, and he is given a wife, Eunoe, who is very similar to Andromache. However, since the activism of Odysseus must ultimately triumph, the play soon becomes a conspiracy between him and the audience against the rest of the cast. Thus Baxter achieves something of the "ironic farce of human vanity" which he admired in Giraudoux,[19] but he failed in his attempt (discernible only in the chorus) to give that irony a contemporary resonance; that is probably why he returned to the problem of locating Greek archetypes within a New Zealand context in two other plays written late in 1967, "The Runaway Wife" and "Mr. O'Dwyer's Dancing Party."

"Mr. O'Dwyer's Dancing Party" is based on Euripides's *Bacchae*, which had already been unsuccessfully modernized in Australian terms.[20] As well as exploiting Euripides, Baxter reworked elements from his own earlier plays "To Catch the Hare" and "The Spots of the Leopard," both of which include a mad Austrian Jew from Auschwitz who finally evolves into the modern Tiresias. O'Dwyer is Dionysus, running an expressive dance group in Auckland among Remuera housewives; O'Dwyer defeats the Pentheus figure in a "pub crawl," and the final scene finds "Tiresias" and "Dionysus" visiting the sedated "Pentheus" in hospital, engaging in a dialogue plagiarized from a poem by Adrian Mitchell.[21]

"The Runaway Wife" was Baxter's first Greek play for which he had no dramatic model, and he approached the Eurydice myth without any prejudicial sense of the value of the kinds of behavior it illustrates; it was deliberately written as a kind of vaudeville, requiring an abstract stage design and the use of masks throughout. Orpheus finds his Eurydice in a coffee bar in Hades, listening to a poetry reading that includes obvious parodies of recognizable Maori poets. The Maori Sisyphus reads a poem attacking "Mouldybroke, Brand and Arsehole," thinly-veiled references to contemporary New Zealand politicians, and the appearance of Mouldybroke on stage achieves a level of mythic irrelevance that the final castration scene cannot correct.

Baxter's last Greek play was an attempt to follow what was probably his earliest dramatic influence, Sartre. His first acting experience was as Second Man in *Les Mouches* in 1948, and he referred to this frequently in his critical writings. In 1967 he read Sartre's adaptation of Euripides' *The Trojan Women;* while he approved of the topicality that Sartre found in Euripides (drawing parallels with the Algerian war), the script focused his attention on his growing conviction that the Greek chorus is intractable on the modern stage.[22] However, discussions with H.D.F. Kitto during his visit to Dunedin led Baxter to reconsider his attitude to the chorus, and the result was *The Temptations of Oedipus*, ostensibly based on Sophocles' *Oedipus at Colonus* but also drawing a good deal from Sartre's *Les Mouches*. Apart from a proliferation of incest in several directions, Baxter kept the general outlines of Sophocles' story, though with a radical revaluation of most characters; as an interplay between the "yogi" (Oedipus) and the "commissar" (Theseus)[23] the play has a gradual but relentless intensification such as Sartre achieved, but is awkwardly oversupplied with machinery for that interplay. The only other named

characters are the children of Oedipus, and these supply an abundance of possibilities for the demonstration of Oedipal behavior
which is resolved very satisfactorily when Antigone's baby is sacrificed at the end. Supporting Theseus's stance is a group of citizens
who are rigidly committed to bureaucratic principles and whose
dialogue frequently echoes Sartre. The children of Oedipus and the
citizens of Theseus give ample social breadth to the interplay of the
main characters.

In addition, however, Baxter chose to use a female chorus. That he
was uncertain of its dramatic function is suggested by the fact that it
does not speak or even receive any stage directions, but he nevertheless insisted that it is conceptually of great importance: the chorus of
furies is a representation of the "chaos" of life, and as such cannot be
allowed the precision of a dramatic role.[24] The presence of the furies
has been a conspicuous embarrassment to most directors of the play
both in practical and in conceptual terms: the nebulous furies seem to
admit Baxter's awareness that a constant weakness in his serious
Greek plays is the absence of any religious or even numinous
determinant.

IV   The False Gods Return to the Stage

In Baxter's plays on New Testament themes the gods are lost,
crosses are confused, and much of the action consists of a search for
the misplaced gods. But in his Greek plays there is not even a concept
of absent gods; "The Bureaucrat," for example, has no equivalent to
the dynamism of Aeschylus's Zeus. Sometimes, characters mention
the gods as if they were the unknown recesses of a bureaucracy, but
the closest Baxter comes to realizing a divine presence is in the trio of
old hags who in several of his plays attempt to castrate the protagonist; they even appear in The Temptations of Oedipus, and this
makes the furies seem even more superfluous.

Ironically, Baxter managed to achieve a more successful treatment
of some of the themes of The Temptations of Oedipus in a much
shorter, non-Greek play which was written toward the end of 1967.
Like The Temptations of Oedipus, "The Starlight in Your Your Eyes"
is set at the entrance to a shelter after a devastating civil war. However, in this play the style is somewhat Brechtian and the setting is in
New Zealand after a nuclear war has destroyed most of the rest of the
world; the country is being run by a fascist called Starlight who is
using his army to bring down the rebellious Moderates, whom he

equates with Communists. Near the start of the play, a mother and her daughter talk to a priest about the war; a wounded Maori Moderate enters and dies after making a confession, and some soldiers try to make the priest reveal the nature of the confession, tying him to a tree and torturing him. The mother attempts to free the priest and is arrested, the priest dies, and a hysterical Catholic soldier is shot; toward the end of the play, the daughter is on stage alone, sobbing, and a Captain enters to explain the war to the audience. "The Starlight in Your Eyes" is generally a well-judged piece of Brechtian drama with vigorously contrapuntal intellectual and emotional elements. Starlight, the ersatz fascist deity in Baxter's parable, posits the existence of a better god.

The Devil and Mr. Mulcahy was written earlier in 1967; its quality was immediately recognized, and yet Baxter made no attempt to write any similar work. Barney Mulcahy, a hard-drinking lapsed Irish Catholic, has some obvious antecedents within Baxter's drama, but the other characters and their ethics are unique. Partly, this is because of the play's factual origin, a North Island murder case in which two boys attempted to kill the rest of their family for misguided religious reasons.[25] Baxter chose to remove the action of his play considerably from his source by the use of a fictitious religion, the "Seed of Light," and thus ensured that audiences would be united in a feeling of alienation toward the religious elitism from which the tragedy arises.

At the start of the play Simon and Rachel, brother and sister, are sitting talking outside the farmhouse. Rural isolation and religious exclusiveness have made their relationship latently incestuous, and Simon's interest in Egyptian myths has made him bold enough to tell his sister of his feelings. Marshall, the patriarchal tyrant, interrupts them, subdues his wife and daughter, and decides that Simon is all that is left to him. Act Two finds Mulcahy, the farmhand, expounding liberal Catholicism to Simon as they work together beside a ditch; Simon is very depressed, and so Mulcahy gives him a cigarette and tells him about a kindhearted barmaid at Temuka, but Marshall enters and dismisses Mulcahy. In the last act the two women talk about their religious constrictions, and Barney comes in and begins to seduce Mrs. Marshall; Simon threatens them with a gun and then shoots his sister offstage, explaining that "She's dead in the Lord."[26] The confusion of taboos in the boy's mind is the source of the tragedy, and Baxter achieves the unveiling of ideological chaos without the invocation of mythic archetypes.

Incest as a response to the claustrophobia of rural puritanism is as appropriate to *The Devil and Mr. Mulcahy* as it is to Eugene O'Neill's *Desire under the Elms*. Baxter described Rachel as "the passive and sacrificed lamb who enables the play to be a ritual happening";[27] elsewhere, he termed Shakespeare's Ophelia "the *tragos*, the sacrificial goat," and suggested that "without a sacrifice of the putatively innocent there is no tragedy."[28] In his Greek plays there is no concept of innocence because there is generally no value system permeating the action. In his alcoholic biblical plays "the Graham Greene law of paradoxical goodness"[29] dictates that guilt and innocence are interchangeable. But in *The Devil and Mr. Mulcahy* and "The Starlight in Your Eyes" the gods are palpably false, and the tyranny of wrong gods allows the sacrifice of the "putatively innocent."

If it is difficult to understand why Baxter wrote no other tragedies of the sacrifice of the "putatively innocent" to false gods, he at least left an explanation of why he never used his own Christian God in a play, insisting that "Human stupidity, not Divine illumination, is the communal foundation of dramatic art."[30] This self-imposed limitation, an evasion of anything that might be termed "truth," governs all of Baxter's writing for the theater, and perhaps explains why a meticulous reviser of poetry seldom attempted to improve a playscript after a premiere.

Technically, there is a great deal of experimentation but little progress to be observed within Baxter's dramatic output, and the influence of the Globe Theatre was not entirely salutary, drawing him into areas of mythological pretension. He always regarded himself as a poet who occasionally wrote a play, and he learned early that when poets write plays their most common mistake is to regard "a given speech as a total poem, not, as it were, as a single unit in the total dramatic poem which is the play."[31] The concept of a play as a "total dramatic poem" employing a collection of the poet's "secret selves" lies implicitly behind all his best work, from *Jack Winter's Dream* (1956) to "The Day that Flanagan Died" (1969), and yet his exploitation of it seems almost accidental, suggesting diffidence about finding and using his "secret selves." Obviously, there is an area of difficulty between the discovery of one's "secret selves" and the location of them within a context of "human stupidity."

Most of Baxter's major plays are of a difficult length and are usually produced as long double bills. Since his death in 1972 revivals within New Zealand have been frequent, but usually limited by excessive fidelity to the script. For his premieres Baxter relied heavily on the resourcefulness of directors like Richard Campion and Patric Carey, and his respect for directorial creativity suggests that the strongest productions will come when his plays are approached like Tennessee Williams's *Camino Real:* as blueprints, not as artifacts.

CHAPTER 6

The Playwrights of the Early 1960s

ETWEEN 1960 and 1965 the New Zealand theater was in a state
of depression, and emergent playwrights were severely hand-
icapped by inadequate production resources. Radio production was
intensifying cautiously, and would flourish later in the decade;
amateur theater was mostly healthy, but had moved into a period of
conservatism following the collapse of the New Zealand Players, so
that only Unity Theatre and the Globe Theatre consistently showed
an adventurous approach to play selection. Unless the local playwright could produce extraordinary credentials, such as success
overseas, his work had little chance of receiving the routine of tryout
productions that is usually behind a polished script. The four playwrights discussed in this chapter would all no doubt have become
much more prominent had they appeared under more favorable
circumstances.

I Stella Jones

The dramatic reputation of Stella Jones rests almost entirely on one
play, *The Tree*. Rejected by numerous local theaters, *The Tree* was
sent overseas and was premiered by The Rapier Players in Bristol in
1957; the New Zealand Players (who had earlier rejected it) sent it on
tour with their second company in 1959, and the New Zealand
Broadcasting Service produced a radio version in 1961. This was a
common pattern: the New Zealand stage was generally interested
only in guaranteed investments, and radio at that time subsisted
largely on adaptations of stage works.

The Tree is a three-act play set around the back porch of the home of
Herbert Willis, a widower in his late sixties. Without appearing
derivative, the action and the situation resemble Arthur Miller's *All
My Sons*: Willis and his twin daughters wait beside the symbolic tree
for the homecoming of the third daughter, who shares, with one of the
twins, the affections of Richard, the man across the road. There the
similarities end, for there are no grand scandals in the world of Stella

76

Jones's characters. The first act establishes a sense of vacuum, uncertainty as to the terms of the family's coherence. The second act clarifies this by taking the action back fifteen years to a point when the girls were still at home, unmarried, and the mother was still alive; immediately, the core of the family is evident in the matriarchal tyranny that subdues them all. In the third act, continuing chronologically from the first, there seems nothing left but for Richard to make his choice; but, by a protraction of the action which is brilliant considering the play's economies, the newly returned daughter reveals herself in her mother's role and the play ends with a strong ambivalence, Richard, the only hope of family solidity, being rejected, perhaps permanently.

The Tree is a play remarkable for its restraint; its power lies in the intensity of its atmosphere, in its tendency toward understatement which activates a subtextual dimension, and in the depth of its female characterization, which James Bertram related to the tradition of Katherine Mansfield and Lady Barker.[1] The same qualities are apparent in Stella Jones's "Between Season," a long radio play completed in 1965.

"Between Season" presents a group of women in an island guest house in late summer. Again, the "vacuum" principle is dominant: Mrs. Watts can talk of nothing but her late husband and married daughters, Christina is in search of extramarital adventure, Miss Castle is aggressively independent of men, and the other characters are all socially dislocated in similar ways. As with *The Tree*, the simple title metaphor reflects the action: the play is an examination of the ageing process and of women's social and biological pressures. Although some of the characters indulge in pretentious philosophizing, the play is of a distinctive quality and is easily stageable.

II *Allen Curnow*

Curnow had firmly established himself as a Christchurch playwright with *The Axe* in 1948, but a substantial break in his writing career followed his shift to Auckland. In 1959 he scandalized much of the Auckland province with "Moon Section," a tragic play described by Sarah Campion as "the first considerable New Zealand play written about the country, its people, and their attitudes, by a New Zealander."[2] Curnow, however, has chosen not to publish the script, and the public reaction to the Community Arts Service tour was such as to make him question the appropriateness of complex naturalistic detail to general New Zealand audiences.

The Overseas Expert was written while "Moon Section" was on its
initial tour, partly as a reaction to public response. *The Overseas
Expert* is a light comedy in free verse set in a Remuera bourgeois
drawing room which admits a good deal of incidental satire. Mona
Soper is preparing a dinner party for Sir George Mandragora, a
visiting English baronet whom Mr. Soper is trying to lure into a
business deal and Gillian Soper is hoping to marry. Bob, the Sopers'
schoolteacher son, arrives home from Northland and immediately
attacks the family pretensions, grounded on a fortune made in pro-
cessing tomato sauce; the women are concerned that Bob seems
likely to embarrass them in the presence of Sir George, who is soon
propelled in by a very drunk Mr. Soper. Bob arouses the audience's
suspicions of George, and these are compounded in the second
scene, after dinner, when George is shown to be borrowing money
from both Mr. Soper and Gillian. The second act begins with Bob
beginning a series of mysterious telephone calls and Gillian arranging
an outing with George; the previous evening they have told the
family of their secret engagement, but now George finds that he must
immediately travel to Australia on business. In the final scene Bob
presents his accumulated evidence that George is a confidence tricks-
ter, which is not denied, but the family has been compromised to
such an extent socially and sexually that George is able to escape to
Australia with a substantial amount of the Sopers' money.

    The Overseas Expert contains a great deal of effective satire against
New Zealand social pretensions and the principle of the "cultural
cringe" which makes overseas expertise always more acceptable than
local resources; the gullibility of New Zealanders in this area is the
pivot of the play's action. *The Overseas Expert* may also be seen as a
contemporary application of principles basic to *The Axe;* Curnow
himself has indicated the similarities between George Mandragora
and the exploitative missionary Davida.[3] However, little of the play's
satire is dramatic in essence, and a number of the longer speeches
illustrate Baxter's opinion that when poets write plays they often
make the mistake of regarding a "given speech as a total poem."[4]
Curnow's reputation as the country's leading verse satirist is long
established, and he offers his patronage rather too overtly in *The
Overseas Expert* to Bob, who describes himself as a bad poet and
frequently moves into satirical verse solos which relate only tangen-
tially to the dramatic situation. As in *The Axe*, Curnow seems more
concerned with abstract forces than with individualized humans, so
that Bob is allowed to become too blatantly the engineer of the

resolution, while the rest of his family becomes the half-comprehending butt of the action.

The Overseas Expert is nevertheless a thoroughly stageworthy play, which was victimized by circumstances in 1959, so that its eventual premiere was on radio in 1961. Curnow, who has stated that theater is "far and away the most profoundly backward and immature of all the arts in New Zealand,"[5] wrote both of his subsequent plays specifically for radio, and an updating of the satire of *The Overseas Expert* for publication in 1972 came too late to improve its acceptability on stage.

James Bertram, who considered that "For the type of subject treated *The Overseas Expert*, Bruce Mason or Joseph Musaphia in plain prose would run rings around our poet," pointed out that Curnow's next play, *The Duke's Miracle* (1966), is essentially "a very *literary* performance."[6] The relationship of Curnow's play to Robert Browning's poem, "My Last Duchess," is complex; the basic situation and characters are derived from Browning, and this is clearly acknowledged, but the play has an autonomy that makes it in no sense a simple dramatization of the poem. The immediate context involves the Duke and the Envoy moving around the Ferrara palace and eventually confronting the portrait of the last duchess, but Curnow inserts a number of earlier scenes governed by the Duke's memory, and introducing the Duchess as an independent character, as well as Fra Pandolf the painter and a number of figures involved in the process of her death. The context of replacing the former duchess is thus amplified, but not made overexplicit, as the enigma of the portrait subject still remains with the Duke; technically, the play is permeated by the powerful irony of a visual subject being explored through an auditory medium.

In another verse play for radio, *Resident of Nowhere* (1969), a similar irony is dominant: James Busby, the historical British Resident of New Zealand who organized a local "Magna Carta" in 1835, reflects on his antipodean enterprises as an old man. The play opens in 1871, with Busby in bed, his eyes heavily bandaged after a cataract operation; the central action of the play is a long series of memory scenes located in New Zealand, and the play ends with Busby's daughter, in New Zealand, receiving news of her father's death. In the central passages of the play the use of verse—and occasionally stylized prose—effectively generates a historically momentous atmosphere, but the use of old Busby as a framing device is not entirely successful; he becomes almost an irrelevancy to the main action, the presentation of which has no overt distortions to remind the listener of the old man's consciousness.

III *Frank Sargeson*

Although Sargeson had attempted dramatic writing in the early 1930s and had shown a continuous interest since then in both dramatic literature and theater, his reputation as a playwright rests on two full-length plays premiered in Auckland in 1961 and 1962 and subsequently adapted for radio.

"If Kendall," wrote the Auckland historian Keith Sinclair in 1959, "awaits his Marlowe or Goethe, Busby (and his superiors) deserves the attention of a Ben Jonson."[7] Within a decade Curnow would have fulfilled the latter commission, but Frank Sargeson was much quicker in stepping into the role of Marlowe: *A Time for Sowing* is a historical study of the missionary Thomas Kendall in the Bay of Islands in 1819, torn between his passionate devotion to Maori culture and the imminent collapse of his European domestic life. Reviewing a preproduction reading of the script, Curnow emphasized the play's naturalism and the related moral and physical inertia,[8] an issue cogently expanded by D. F. McKenzie: "Mr. Sargeson's characters are, alas, all too credible, but the potentially pathetic dispersion of Kendall's mind, failing in its alcoholic negritophilia to focus on any possible issue, could only be tragic had Mr. Sargeson shown in every strand of his art that this was—figuratively of course—*his* problem too."[9]

The dramaturgic flaw of the play consists in selecting largely internalized issues such as Kendall's self-doubt and attempting to articulate these issues through essentially naturalistic techniques. Moreover, the play's audiences knew that Kendall's life was not by any means as static as Sargeson's play suggested; it was Kendall who took Hongi (the subject of Mason's play) to England in 1820, who seduced a remarkable cross section of the local Maori population, and who was recalled in disgrace by the Church Missionary Society. Kendall, as a practical pioneer of modern anthropology, would be an excellent subject for naturalistic drama, but Sargeson's play does not illustrate this facet of his character.

A partial solution to these problems might have come through fictionalizing the characters, as Sargeson has done in novels like *The Hangover.* His next play, *The Cradle and the Egg* (1962), shows no signs of factual origins and presents problems of a quite different order. The three acts are set in a New Zealand township in the 1880s, in an aeroplane over the Pacific in the 1950s, and on a rock in space at some later time. The same central characters occur in the last two acts: an explosion on the aeroplane has, it appears, blown three of its occupants into eternity. The one character linking the first two acts is an old man on the aeroplane who was a baby in the first act and who does not appear on the rock. The incidental felicities of this Shavian drama are numerous, but its coherence, depending on cradle and egg symbolism, literary allusion (to Anthony Trollope and Oscar Wilde), and various philosophies of time, is crudely contrived. In technical terms the play is considerably more ambitious than *A Time for Sowing*, particularly in the attempt to use visual expression as a vital function of the play's total meaning, but the New Zealand stage in 1962 did not offer the facilities for a playwright to learn from his mistakes.

IV   *Campbell Caldwell*

Unity Theatre had mounted the earliest stage plays of both Bruce Mason and James K. Baxter. In 1962 it introduced another full-length playwright with a premiere season of Campbell Caldwell's "Flowers Bloom in Summer" in the Wellington Concert Chamber. The play made its initial impact by the breadth of its social panorama, following a schoolteacher's attempts to preserve a responsible and progressive approach to his work in a small North Island town where racial feelings are strong. The action culminates in a stormy scene at the start of the third act in which a vote of confidence in the teacher is eventually passed. However, for the teacher the issue has become obscured by his personal relationships, which are not as plausibly presented, and the schoolroom scene is followed by an anticlimactic rendezvous with a girl who works at the local store; a final scene, in which the teacher tentatively restores domestic harmony, has an incongruous tone of ambivalence for a play that seems to have established a more severe patterning of action.

"After the Wedding" (1964) showed a considerable refinement of technique in its essentially realistic examination of New Zealand married life, and in its 1965 revival activated undercurrents of audience self-consciousness remarkably similar to the response to Bruce Mason's "The Evening Paper" in the same year. "After the Wedding" has dated fast because the instrumentation of such realism is highly transitory; the play that shocked some audiences in the mid-1960s seemed generally mannered by the end of the decade, but the playwright lacked the facilities to experiment with subtleties of audience manipulation in a less ephemeral mode.

"The Prisoners" (1967) involves a group of predominantly New Zealand prisoners of war in Germany late in 1944. The introduction of a suspected informer into their barracks brings numerous tensions to the surface; after a brutal interrogation, the informer confesses and escapes. The scene, however, results in another character admitting his sadistic proclivities; he reminisces about New Zealand farm life and departs, to be killed in an escape attempt. The mechanics of the play are crude, but in terms of its dated genre the work is strong, particularly in characterization, and suggests an author maturing too slowly to keep pace with audience requirements.

Nola Millar, who had directed Caldwell's first three plays for Unity Theatre, chose her own New Theatre in Wellington for the premiere of "A Southerly Wind"[10] in 1973, which was to be one of her last productions before her death. The play is set in the living room of a Wairarapa runholder (a sheep farmer with a very large farm), with the expectation of the family converging for Christmas. The runholder, his partner wife, their poet son, their pregnant daughter, the bank manager, an inventor, and various other characters become isolated overnight by flood, and the daughter going into labor precipitates a series of crises; normality is restored when the baby is born, the house is continued by the birth of a new generation, and the electricity is restored. Like Caldwell's other plays, "A Southerly Wind" pivots on vital involuntary causation, so that much of the central action seems blatantly contrived.

Campbell Caldwell emerged at a time when the New Zealand playwright was, of necessity, an autodidact. But whereas numerous other writers took advantage of new production opportunities in the mid-1960s to increase their technical resourcefulness, Caldwell remained true to a style of theater that has become less acceptable since the advent of television.

CHAPTER 7

The Playwrights of the Late 1960s

NO single event can account for the spectacular intensification of New Zealand playwriting since the mid-1960s, although vital influences lay in the progressive policies of the New Zealand Broadcasting Corporation, in the production approaches of Downstage Theatre and the various professional community theaters that followed it, and in the restructuring and coordination of amateur theater. The New Zealand Theatre Federation incorporated the New Zealand branch of the British Drama League and the New Zealand Drama Council, while the professional theaters formed the Association of Community Theatres, the New Zealand branch of the International Theatre Institute. In the same period the Queen Elizabeth II Arts Council of New Zealand developed a training and subsidy system (which made the New Zealand Players' deficits look negligible), and the emergence of the New Zealand television industry considerably expanded production opportunities. All of these factors meant that there was greater demand and competitive remuneration for local playscripts, as well as a variety of outlets that encouraged technical experimentation.

In the early 1960s two remarkable young writers had emerged relatively unobtrusively, both of whom were to make important contributions to New Zealand drama after learning the potential of the radio medium: Joseph Musaphia and Warren Dibble. Musaphia was to achieve his greatest popularity with his stage work in the 1970s (and will be discussed in that context), but Dibble withdrew from New Zealand literary activity at what seemed to be the peak of his early maturity.

I Warren Dibble

Warren Dibble first became widely known as a writer with two very short stories in *Landfall* in 1968;[1] his reputation grew rapidly, and two years later he was granted the Burns Fellowship at the University of Otago, even though his published output was very slender. In fact, Dibble had established himself as a competent and resourceful radio dramatist as early as 1962.

"Loser on Drums" (1962) is a sensitive study of a subnormal mentality, revolving around a boy whose ambition is to become a jazz drummer. The quality of the characterization is a central strength to the play, but Dibble's technical resourcefulness in this first play is remarkable; as well as cross-fading among numerous locations and through time, he represents the boy's delirium toward the end expressionistically, with a building going on fire and a montage of flashback voices from earlier in the play. Also, Dibble capitalizes on the absence of concrete location in radio: in places, the voices retreat into a vague limbo, which appropriately represents the boy's mind.

For his next play, "The Man who Chopped His Finger Off" (1963), Dibble built a pub yarn into the structure of a dramatized memory sequence which occupies most of the play, with an ironic twist at the end that reveals the whole thing as a lie. In production, a sixty-eight-minute play like this usually needs more than the single interlude that Dibble provides to maintain the narrative presence, but, again, the play is supported by subtlety of characterization; the narrator (who is also the main character in the memory sequence) is a very engaging figure, a garrulous "rough diamond."

"Breakthrough" (1965) follows a young Maori on a two-year prison sentence; the style is episodic and directionless, and the ending has an awkward tone of didacticism. However, in another play of the same year Dibble experimented more successfully with disorientation as a theme. "A Recital" involves a Man and a Lady who live through a vague fantasy together; she is to do a recital of some arias but has forgotten where it is to be held, and they walk around the streets in a nostalgic, make-believe mood, talking about their past. They have apparently been friends for some time, but cannot remember whether they have ever been lovers. The relevance of their conversation becomes secondary to their reliability, which in turn calls their independent existence into question; the play's coherence shifts from an attempt to trace logical causation to a search for their identity. They go into a church, and she decides to sing her aria there, but does not; there is a long silence. There is a fade to later that afternoon; the Lady is speaking to the Man, who does not answer. The play ends with the Lady reading from the Bible; the Man's presence is in doubt, and this in turn throws doubt on his existence as an autonomous character throughout the play. "A Recital" is an audacious play which shows an important technical advance: it is the first work in New Zealand radio drama to make a virtue of the absence of a visual dimension.

"A Recital" is an exciting play to the specialist, but scarcely one to appeal to general audiences, and in the next two years Dibble attempted to accommodate technical experimentation within more conventional narratives. "Carnovan" (1966) is about a South African headmaster attempting to drown himself while on holiday in Auckland; much of the action is internal, with dramatized memory sequences and numerous episodes of conversation with a nonexistent, expressionistic Examiner. Also, in 1966–67, Dibble began writing for stage and for television, most successfully with " The Killing of Kane" (1967), a Maori historical play for television. However, technical enterprise also brought his career as a television dramatist to a halt: in 1966 he wrote *How With This Rage*, a "television play without dialogue,"[2] which was bought by the New Zealand Broadcasting Corporation but never produced, possibly because of its unfavorable attitude toward the New Zealand Army, whose assistance was needed for the supply of helicopters and explosives. The absence of words in *How With This Rage* does not parallel the absence of image in "A Recital"; in the television play there is so little attention to characterization that dialogue would be superfluous to the indulgence in a series of images, and the absence of dialogue is not used significantly to exploit mystery.

Dibble's first work for the stage appears to have been *"Lord, Dismiss Us . . .",* which won the all-women section of the British Drama League playwriting competition in 1966. The stereotyped nature of this play may be explained as an attempt to conform with the kind of play that normally won such prizes. Set in the headmistress's study of a girls' college, it involves an attempt to discipline a recalcitrant pupil who has been reading erotic literature; it ends with the girl, who has been very defiant, breaking down and sobbing by herself. George Webby, reviewing the Downstage Theatre production, observed that the play "would be of little more than routine interest if it hadn't been followed by the extraordinary *Lines to M*,"[3] which he considered the best New Zealand play he had ever seen.

"Lord, Dismiss Us . . ." and *Lines to M* were presented as a double bill both at Downstage Theatre in 1969 and on New Zealand radio in 1966. The former was obviously conceived as a work for the stage, in which Dibble clumsily attempted to translate a simple element of radio technique (elastic time) into a different medium. In 1967 he referred to *Lines to M* as a stage play that had been adapted for radio,[4]

and the published script shows a remarkable fusion of radio and stage methods.

The pattern of *Lines to M* involves a simple alternation of soliloquy and dialogue. The soliloquy is generally delivered from a lectern, which is itself a deliberate attempt at visual deprivation, and the dialogue only once involves more than two people; thus there is the effect of dialogue being generated from soliloquy, as happened on radio in "A Recital," and as the play develops so does one's impression that the existence of the dialogue is masochistically governed by the soliloquy. As in "A Recital," Dibble teases the audience with a complex problem of causation which finally dissolves into a question of identity and reliability; here, the problem is more elaborate, and the clues are accordingly more lavishly supplied.

At the start of *Lines to M*, the character of Victor Spilman is established, in soliloquy to the audience, as that of a sad, somewhat pedantic, middle-aged man with an absurdly meticulous sense of detail and numerous nervous mannerisms. After a very factual description of his life, he suddenly offers the information that within the last year he murdered his daughter. This statement activates a labyrinth of causation, revolving around why he murdered her and how his present condition relates to the murder; his location is completely undefined, so that he could be in prison, in an afterlife, in hiding, or virtually anywhere. Moreover, his character has been established as the most reliable, objective of narrators, and so the audience is drawn into scanning the information he offers, confident that nothing will be overlooked. Using a blackboard diagram, Spilman commits himself to the same enquiry, and a draughts game with a neighbor reveals nothing about the murder but lays the grounds for Spilman's unreliability, not noticed at the time because of the distraction of a detection situation. Another soliloquy takes Spilman into a scene in which he is teaching the cello to a girl; there is a power failure, another soliloquy, and a scene in which the girl's mother tells Spilman she has informed the police that he interfered with her daughter during the power failure. Alone, Spilman talks about the "prosecution of the imagination," and then discusses the coming trial with his neighbor; it is clear that Violet, his daughter, is still alive. But guilt, by this stage, has become ambiguous, as has the "prosecution of the imagination." Spilman seems to transfer the alleged guilt of violating his pupil to his assumed guilt of murdering his daughter, and the imagination begins overtly to color his soliloquy; there is uncertainty about whether the slightly incestuous tone comes from a confusion of the two girls or whether there is a real connection between the violation and the murder.

In a courtroom episode the neighbor is questioned by a barrister, who gives a long final speech for both the defense and the prosecution, an antiphonal projection of Spilman's own confusion. Told he is not guilty, he replies that perhaps he is not, and suggests to the audience that the "M" of the title might stand for "Mistake" and not for "Murder." By this stage, his reliability as a narrator is very much in doubt. There is a scene in which he is beaten up by the brother of the girl he allegedly violated, and he telephones a woman, asking her to take care of Violet while he recovers. His final soliloquy becomes progressively more frenzied; he reveals that Violet was killed in a car crash that afternoon, he demonstrates that by telephoning the woman he committed murder, and, with the stage in total darkness, his soliloquy dissolves into furious apocalyptic shouts.

One never knows where the events of *Lines to M* happen; in fact, one never knows *if* they happen. By manipulating the audience's instinctive desire to find a causal connection among the events in a narrative, Dibble elicits deep sympathy with the workings of a deranged mind, and because the outcome of that derangement is an obsessional preoccupation with responsibility and causation the play offers a profound character study while at the same time parodying some theater conventions. The element of parody is only possible because the level of realism is continuously in doubt, and Dibble uses most of the visual devices, such as the classroom situation and the schizoid barrister, not for intensifying visual illusion but virtually for the opposite: first, the action is deprived of a dimension in time, then the illusion of visual realism is shattered, and finally the action is reduced to an existence in the mind alone. Such a pattern of reduction is similar to that in "A Recital," except that by his exploitation of the resources of live theater in *Lines to M* Dibble gave it much greater scope and impact.

During his tenure of the Burns Fellowship, Dibble did some acting and writing for the Globe Theatre, but since then seems to have lost interest in dramatic writing.

II *Alexander Guyan*

Like Joseph Musaphia, Alexander Guyan first drew attention to himself with a stage play in the early 1960s and then moved to radio drama. The prologue of *Conversations with a Golliwog* (1962) finds Canny, a very precocious fourteen-year-old, in dialogue with Boswell, a very articulate golliwog. For the three acts that make up the central part of the play, Boswell is inanimate, and what action there is revolves around Canny; she is now aged nineteen and, with a constant alternation of childish petulance and sophisticated bad language, she dominates her mother, her brother, and her boyfriend. Finally, she breaks down, and the epilogue finds her in hospital, once again in conversation with Boswell. The golliwog motif is an effective way of projecting the girl's impasse between regression and precociousness, but Guyan's use of it is scarcely sufficient to sustain the continuity of the whole play. Consequently, attention focuses on the person (rather than the projection) of Canny, whose vitality and recalcitrance offer a continuous supply of humorous dialogue; however, since almost all of this humor is generated by a simple incongruity, the play's final acts appear technically self-conscious.

Conversations with a Golliwog was accepted for radio in 1964, as was Guyan's next play, *Modern Man at Breakfast*, which was also originally written for the stage; it is an undistinguished domestic farce concerning a woman's machinations to get rid of her husband because she is pregnant to the vicar. Four other very short plays date to the same year, all conceived essentially in stage terms. "Nothing and Everything and a Woman with a Pram" is an existentialist sketch about two old men in a park, and "Billy Coming Home" is about a family waiting for Billy, who has just finished a three-year jail sentence; both plays illustrate Guyan's limited powers of characterization. However, his comic work of the same period showed more promise and derived more directly from his experience in scripting student revues: *The Projectionist*[5] is about an old projectionist who, on the verge of death, is visited by the film characters of his youth, and "Klapman Flies" made a good outlet for Guyan's iconoclastic humor in its placing of a cynic in an airport lounge waiting for a delayed flight. All of these plays received radio production in 1965. In the same year Guyan wrote a stereotyped comic fantasy, "The Magicians," and, returning to the more serious level of *Conversations with a Golliwog*, "Pop Goes the Rat," a portrait of a nasty young pop singer in which he achieved his best characterization to date. Structurally, "Pop Goes the Rat" is a simple narrative, but in "The Arrangement for Thursday" (1966) he attempted a much more adventurous radio technique.

"The Arrangement for Thursday" starts with an Old Man soliloquizing about how he will kill a Young Man, who soon enters; the Old Man is at first obsequious but, with a sudden change of tone, forces the Young Man into a cellar. Apparently forgetting everything, the Old Man then rescues him, gives him a drink, and tells him how he murdered his wife. The play becomes more complex, and after several more abortive murder attempts the Young Man is taken away by a policeman, apparently to an asylum. The Old Man then locks a girl in the cellar; it seems that she is his daughter and that the Young Man is his son, but the play ends with the characters and their relationships only vaguely defined. Through the exploitation of this vagueness, which is particularly easy to achieve on radio, Guyan develops an atmosphere of menace and claustrophobia, but the play as a whole seems amorphous because of the absence of any human element that the audience can attach itself to for any length of time; both the main characters are so protean that there is inevitably a failure of perspective.

Since 1967 Guyan has mostly confined himself to lighter work, mainly farce and the whimsical treatment of romantic themes. In 1967 he wrote a farce, "The Man Who Knew Almost Everything"; a domestic drama adapted from one of his own stories, "Happiness is a Horse"; and an insubstantial romantic play, "Do You Love Me? Of Course I Do." He expanded a similar love relationship for his first television play, "Flowers and Coffins" (1970), and contracted the material again to a very simple boy-meets-girl situation for his second television play, "Lunch with Richard Burton" (1973).

It is not easy to account for Guyan's popularity, or for the approval he has found from critics with a reputation for high standards: Bruce Mason, Margaret Dalziel, David Hall, and Charles Brasch were all very much in support of *Conversations with a Golliwog* and "Lunch with Richard Burton" was judged the best New Zealand television play of the year.[6] Certainly, Guyan can show a sophisticated and idiosyncratic sense of humor, and he has developed some skills of characterization and construction. But his output as a whole seems to reflect a gradual lowering of dramatic ambitions which has meant that the promise seen in his first play has not been amply fulfilled.

III *Mark Richards*

The year of Guyan's radio début, 1964, also marked the establishment of a number of other radio dramatists, including Mark Richards, Dora Somerville, Alistair Campbell, and Julian Dickon. Of these, Dickon has shown the greatest persistence and professionalism; at the other extreme, Richards was very prolific for about two years and then apparently retired from radio drama.

Apart from a short farce, "A Comprehensive Cover" (1966), the distinguishing quality of all Mark Richards's radio plays is that they are in verse. Since his work also shows a remarkable range of subject matter, it seems that he considered verse a suitable medium for any theme, but his practice would scarcely support such an opinion. "Starfall" is a ninety-minute melodrama about rocket research in which crude verse seems to be used to compensate for weaknesses of dialogue, and "The Premier's New Missile" is a futuristic variant on the "Emperor's New Clothes" motif. "Alpha and Omega" is about the creation of Adam and Eve, and "A Burnt Child" is a drama about cave men. In these plays verse may have been employed to give their language a neutrality of register, but the naïveté of their story-lines imposes its own constrictions on the use of language. Probably Richards's only successful radio play is "Odysseus," a two-hour verse adaptation which effectively uses an inner-voice technique to confront Odysseus.

IV *Dora Somerville*

The work of Mark Richards is of interest mainly because it seems to develop from premises similar to those of Dora Somerville's early plays, which appear to attempt to compensate for a general naïveté of conception by the use of pretentious and allusive language, sometimes verse. From the start her work showed an excessive self-consciousness about the radio medium. In "Agape" (1964) eight people jump into a cellar and give themselves Greek letters for names; expecting a nuclear attack, they form an encounter group and explain their backgrounds until a caretaker rescues them and tells them that the news of a nuclear attack was just a play on the radio. "Visit" (1965) treats the same idea as Dibble's "A Recital," with two very similar characters, but the man's absence is acknowledged by a dream sequence on echo toward the end. "Commonplace Quadrille" (1965) involves a Roving Radio Reporter visiting families and producing "a chamber quartet for radio," and "March Back" (1967) follows a man's reactions to a radio report that scientists have managed to make dogs and mice breathe under water. Of this play Eric Bradwell observed:

"Like much of Mrs. Somerville's work, "March Back" was more concerned with ideas than with dramatic form, and her preoccupation with metaphysics, to the exclusion of logical dramatic development, gave the play an untidy structure. I always find this author's work intriguing, even if at times its meaning is not crystal clear, and in this instance there were times when I suspected that the author was using words more for her own emotional satisfaction than as a means of developing her thesis in a disciplined manner.[7]

The same comment could be made of another play of the same year, "Double Fugue," which starts as a domestic drama until an old man gives everyone LSD and precipitates a situation in which poetical flights can move in an undisciplined manner.

Bradwell's estimation was confirmed by "The Sculptor and the Lady" (1971), a modern variation on the theme of Pygmalion and Galatea, of which a critic found that "the dialogue and the characters sometimes appeared to add up to a private joke."[8] The self-indulgence of private jokes, conceits, and recondite allusions has vitiated most of Somerville's work and obscured simple narrative structures like "The Dilemma of Futura Jet" (1974) and "Joe's Story" (1975). Of the Downstage Theatre production of "One Man Goon" (1969), which she termed "a contrived happening," George Webby wrote: "Somewhat like the old-style vaudevillian who would use a walking-stick in a variety of ways, as a gun, a golf club, a trumpet, and so on, [the actor] uses a foam-rubber mock-up of a pair of women's breasts, although what their significance was in this context eluded me. I refuse to believe they were the obvious reasons, for nothing Miss Somerville does is ever obvious."[9] Otherwise, the play was found hackneyed and shapeless, which is the more remarkable as it was a contribution to a prominent season of New Zealand plays.

Dora Somerville's best work is generally agreed to be *Maui's Farewell* (1966), a verse monologue which has been performed on stage and on radio. Not in any overt way a dramatic script, it was as a literary achievement that it was warmly praised by critics such as James K. Baxter.[10] Preoccupation with verbal dexterity obviously has often meant disregard for dramatic form, and the best evidence of Somerville's dramatic ability is in two plays, scripted for both radio and stage, in which her tangential propensities are channelled into nonverbal areas. "Equivocal Generation" (1971) has twenty-eight scenes punctuated by miscellaneous taped effects, and "The Treasurer" (1972) calls for fifty-two scenes and a heterogeneous collection of slides which are projected intermittently throughout the play. In both plays Somerville's allusive energies seem to have been spent on the technical effects, and, if these are ignored, one finds two simple domestic dramas with a well-shaped story-line, a subtle but accessible sense of humor, and some very competent dialogue, especially among adolescent characters.

The radio plays of Dora Somerville and Mark Richards mark an extremity in New Zealand radio drama, in which the playwrights seem to be aiming at complexity and sophistication as ends in themselves. Behind both playwrights there seems to be a concept of radio as an elitist medium; Somerville, for instance, generally assumes that listeners are fully conversant with literature, mythology, and the arts. The plethora of allusion, wordplay, and self-conscious naïveté seems to be offered almost in apology for the limitations of radio, and this contrasts sharply with the exploitation of those limitations which, already observed in Dibble, has become a very strong tendency among more recent radio playwrights.

V Alistair Campbell

As a radio playwright, Alistair Campbell began with some obvious advantages as an established poet and editor. He experimented with the possibilities of radio drama in *Sanctuary of Spirits* (1963), and he was under no obligation to prove himself as a writer, as may be suspected of some of his radio contemporaries.

Sanctuary of Spirits evolved, in Campbell's drafts, from a "play for radio" to "a tone poem for voices," and from there to its final published form as "a pattern of voices,"[11] reflecting its dramatic origins only vestigially. The ostensible action concerns the historical Maori chief Te Rauparaha who in the years around 1830 committed numerous large-scale atrocities, sometimes with European assistance; however, the basic action consists of the diachronic conflict between an implied authorial figure and the Te Rauparaha principle. Campbell is of Scottish and Polynesian ancestry, and has acknowledged that the work was autobiographical in origin, an attempt to "exorcise" the Polynesian past and "to come to terms with . . . the dark side of" himself.[12]

The technical evolution of *Sanctuary of Spirits* is too complex to be adequately represented by a brief description, but generally involved a gradual reduction of conventional objective characterization into a fluid texture of voices, most of which are only momentarily individualized before dissolving again into their amorphous collective context. The presidency of the authorial synthesizing mind is the single shaping device governing the action, which in the final section condenses into a confrontation between Te Rauparaha and the implied author located within the poet's mind. *Sanctuary of Spirits* has obvious thematic similarities to Curnow's *The Axe*, but achieves much greater dramatic resonance; Curnow observes the conflict of elemental forces from a very safe perspective, but Campbell finds himself caught between those forces, the victim of a divided autobiographical identity which he is able to dramatize overtly.

For his first orthodox radio play, "The Homecoming" (1964), Campbell took events from his own diary, and, through the use of flashbacks, accommodated them into a single afternoon. At the start of the play Robert Metekingi receives a telephone call from his wife, Kate, inviting him to come home; it is obvious that their marriage is in a state of disharmony, partly because of their different racial backgrounds. Robert gets on a train to go home, and the homecoming occupies the rest of the play, with the frequent interpolation of his dramatized thought sequences, mostly connected with his wife. The audience is held largely by a problem of causation, but since Robert also shares the problem the quality of the characterization is vital to the play's success. Also, there is a deliberate vagueness about the location in time of the dramatized thought sequences; the chronology of Robert's memory is elusive, and in places there is uncertainty as to whether his thoughts present memory or hypothesis.

As a presentation of the complex background of what appears to be a commonplace domestic situation, the play is very successful. But Campbell was trying to do more than that:

I try to suggest some of the pressures that most people are up against today, mostly to do with conformity. Kate and Robert have different backgrounds, attitudes and races. Forces in the forms of parental influence, conventions and prejudices pull Kate one way and her love for Robert pulls her another. He, of course, refuses to change or adapt to her, and the result is catastrophic. The play illustrates—and illustration is needed—the hazards involved in marrying an Outsider. [13]

In fact, the play does not manage to illustrate that. Campbell intended to present Kate as "a sensitive, warm human being . . . who finds reality so complex, harsh, and uncompromising that she retreats into mental illness," [14] but because of the subjectivity of the narration Kate is allowed little independent existence and can command no sympathy.

Although ostensibly very different in content, Campbell's next play also attempts the dramatic exploitation of subjectivity without limiting the work as a whole to a private vision. Campbell wrote "The Proprietor" (1965) immediately after seeing Eugène Ionesco's *Exit the King* at the Downstage Theatre, and he was consciously attempting to emulate Ionesco's comic style, although he also acknowledges the influence of the Marx Brothers, the Keystone Cops, and the Goon Show. [15] Whatever its stylistic origins, the content of "The Proprietor" is very much Campbell's own. A group of characters with vaguely Greek names meet in what is apparently a guest house with eccentric features like a cow in the broom cupboard; this vein of zany humor is continuous throughout the play. The dramatic structure consists in the gradual dissolution of every constant element in the environment, beginning with the exterior location: the view becomes a scene, and it changes on the whim of a scene-shifter. The interior turns into a farm, then into a road; the appearance of cars introduces the fluidity of time as well as space, so that movement through space can constitute movement backwards and forwards through time. By this stage the play seems to be developing its own logic, and the Greek elements seem to be taking on a sharper definition with the implication that travel through time has taken the play into the world of Greek myth. However, Campbell simply uses this idea to disguise the fact that the location is assuming the form of a hospital, and the play ends with the abrupt realization that the main character is screaming out for his wife Persephone from his bed in a mental hospital.

In *Sanctuary of Spirits* there is a deliberate obscurity about where the real dramatic confrontation is taking place, an obscurity which is developed by a careful exploitation of the resources of radio and which is resolved by the presentation of a synthesizing mind toward the end. This is precisely what happens in "The Proprietor" also: obscurity of location is at first used for innocuous comic purposes, but as the rationale is inflated to grotesque proportions so does the play's vision become more personalized. To the man in the asylum, the play's components are revealed as antagonists in an inner landscape, just as Te Rauparaha in *Sanctuary of Spirits* becomes a predator in search of the poet's core of identity. The poet's final cry to Te Rauparaha, *"Madman, leave me alone!"*, [16] also echoes through the ending of "The Proprietor."

For *The Suicide* (1965) Campbell used only two characters, explaining their function in an introductory note: "Adam Jones and Jonesy are the conflicting sides of the same person. Adam should have the typical educated New Zealand accent, and Jonesy the Kiwi accent, except when he slips into other roles."[17] The principle was scarcely novel even when Eugene O'Neill used it, but Campbell adapted it to his own preoccupations. At the start, Adam, the inner self, is approached by Jonesy, who is at first pleasant but becomes aggressive. Even though Adam does not know him, Jonesy's regional identity gives him a claim to be present; in this sense Jonesy parallels the Te Rauparaha of *Sanctuary of Spirits*, both of them invaders of the sanctuary, but not without some territorial rights. Adam sets off on the most herculean gymnastics through time and space in an attempt to dislodge Jonesy, who is alternately aggressive and overfamiliar, and whose persecution assumes various stereotyped roles. Goon Show radio techniques are in evidence throughout the play, especially in the use of footstep effects, and the whole work would be little more than a surrealist escape story were it not for an inversion of perspective at the end: the two figures switch roles, and the purpose changes from escape to self-destruction.

In *The Suicide* Campbell used the same approach as in "The Homecoming," that of presenting the "synthesizing mind" at the start, and saved the work from the limitations of complete subjectivity only by the schizoid nature of that mind, which enables such an inversion to occur at the end. But in "The Death of the Colonel" (written in 1966 but unproduced) the surrealist effects are all just a projection of the insane colonel who is presented at the start; consequently, there is no room for formal development.

After the rejection of "The Death of the Colonel" Campbell retired from radio drama, returning only with "The Wairau Incident" (1969), a historical play about one of the massacres that Te Rauparaha was involved in. Concern for historical accuracy, however, reduces the vigor of the characterization considerably.

As early as 1965 Campbell had decided to write a stage version of "The Homecoming,"[18] and in 1967 he himself directed a one-act treatment for a British Drama League festival. In 1969 he was commissioned by William Austin (best known as director of radio drama) to write a stage play for Downstage Theatre, and he again turned to "The Homecoming." This time, he chose to present the whole action from the angle of Kate rather than Robert (whom he renamed Matt), and abandoned chronology completely. The stage play, entitled *When the Bough Breaks*, starts and finishes with a clock striking three, and the whole action revolves around Kate's bed in a mental hospital, a motif Campbell retained from "The Proprietor" and "The Death of the Colonel." The main dramaturgic problem thus became the projection of Kate's delirium, and in this Campbell worked in association with the director, Phillip Mann. To establish the absence of chronology and the essential unreality of the delirium, they decided to locate the play in a neutral space, defined by light only, and the reduction of visual realism was further intensified by sharing the eleven minor characters among only three actors, using only an essential prop to indicate a change in function.

In the first scene Kate is alone in hospital. She calls for Matt and he appears; but instead of paying attention to her he is seducing another girl. This treatment of isolation recurs throughout the play; in her loneliness Kate calls up another person, but when that person turns out to be uncooperative, indifferent, or antagonistic she tries to move back into her isolation. The retreat into mental illness, which Campbell had attempted to portray in "The Homecoming," is here vividly expressed.

But if the expressionistic structure of *When the Bough Breaks* were employed just to present a confused memory it would be governed by the same subjectivity as "The Homecoming," and, since the quality of Kate's mind is exposed at the start, its reliability could not be used as a dramatic variable as Dibble had done in *Lines to M.* However, Campbell counterweights this subjectivity by his presentation of Matt, who appears so reasonable when he visits Kate in hospital in the second scene that he makes a conflicting claim on the audience's sympathy which gradually turns into alienation toward Kate. The inner sanctuary is, again, overrun by the invading spirit; but sympathy with the invader is a new development, and Matt's position is consolidated further. After a soliloquy that emphasizes Kate's unreliability, two memory scenes of courtship, and two scenes in the hospital, there is a scene in which Kate does not appear, so that Matt's existence develops an independence. Then, in the following scene, Matt recites a well-known Alistair Campbell poem as his own, and Kate joins in the last verse. Whether the audience knows the poem or not, the effect is of overt authorial synthesis, providing the first real ground for harmony between the characters.

The rest of the play consists mainly of memory scenes that may be real or hypothetical, generally governed by Kate's delirium, but with Matt or a poem sometimes taking control. The play ends with Kate, like the main character of "The Proprietor," screaming out that she has lost her mind and that she is in hell, but her conclusion has been anticipated by the poems; their theme has developed from innocence to the Fall, and from there to chaos, mental collapse, and isolation.[19] Campbell has said that he used the poems to lift the play beyond the "purely personal,"[20] and the play thus generalizes the concept of sanctuary and exploits it for formal cohesion while retaining the privileged subjectivity of the poet's perspective.

VI *Peter Bland*

When Alistair Campbell wrote his plays, he was employed in the School Publications branch of the Department of Education, where he worked with several other New Zealand playwrights including

Baxter. Campbell's success in turn encouraged Peter Bland, another employee, to begin writing plays.

Peter Bland was one of the founders of Downstage Theatre, and in its first year of activity he was involved as an administrator, director, actor, and revue writer. But Bland was best known as a poet, praised by Baxter for his "aggression": "An immigrant from modern England, Bland is never much haunted by pieties of land and habitation. He is able to see New Zealand society much as it is: an uninspiring offshoot from the tree of Western civilisation, in which the sap has never been very green."[21]

As a playwright, Bland became most popular as a comedian, but in view of the preoccupations of his poetry it is not surprising that his first play is a basically serious study of a tense domestic situation. *Father's Day* was produced as a three-act stage play at Downstage Theatre in 1966, with a forty-minute radio version following almost immediately. Set in the living room of a state house, it involves a woman in her early sixties who has been deserted by her husband, and her two pregnant daughters, one of whom is married. All of them are hypersensitive about their conditions, although to start with the daughters conceal their feelings better than their mother; the imminence of Father's Day, however, precipitates an explosive situation, and by the end of the play the married daughter has succumbed to her mother's paranoid sense of persecution.

Father's Day is remarkable as a first play for the high quality of its naturalistic dialogue, characterization, and incidental comedy, but its lack of shape is emphasized by its extensive abridgment and rearrangement as a radio script. One of Bland's central purposes is to show that for his characters life is repetitious, but the audience realizes this very quickly, and the dramatic action loses interest. However, this weakness was overcome in his next play, *George the Mad Ad-Man* (1967), a half-hour comedy with serious undertones. George, an advertising photographer, arrives home with a model, intending to do an evening's work, a situation which is blithely accepted by his wife. But George is somewhat overtaxed by his work, and as his wife and the model exchange roles a feeling arises that this is a projection of George's confusion. The play ends with George, having tried unsuccessfully to shoot and strangle the model, dissolving in maniacal laughter. Bland has said that he "had to prune down the play to just the comedy situation and no social comment,"[22] but the play does contain serious implications, and one critic justly observed that it "is full of uproarious but sweet-sour lines and situations that have much of importance to say about marriage, illusion, reality, and human fulfillment."[23]

In the same year Bland wrote his first work specifically for radio, *Shsh! He's Becoming a Republic.* Like Dora Somerville's early work, it begins self-consciously with a radio interview situation: George Gabriel, having bought a state house from the New Zealand Government, has declared himself a republic, and is being questioned on the implications of his action. The play involves a number of dramatized memory and fantasy episodes, the tone of which fluctuates between farce and satire; however, as Gabriel's credibility collapses, so do the serious implications of the situation, and the play emerges as a very well written, but completely inconsequential, farce. This play has also proved popular on stage.

Before his return to England in 1968 Bland wrote several short works for stage and television, but his only other substantial work appears to have been an autobiographical radio play, "I'm Off Now." Bland has described how the play developed out of a series of his poems: "The emphasis is on a poetic use of colloquial language together with the imaginative recollection of the local scene. Radio is the ideal medium for both of these purposes . . . The most personal sharing of mood and feeling can be interwoven with the very landscape out of which those feelings grew. This is why "I'm Off Now" is a radio play—it is a medium in which both the poetic and the dramatic can still be worked as a unity."[24] Bland's intentions offer an interesting commentary on the radio drama of poets like Baxter and Campbell, but his play is only a partial success. About half its duration is devoted to the comments of the narrator, a seventeen-year-old North Country lad; various episodes fade into "the echo chamber or electronic sound appropriate to the inner landscape of Narrator's own mind."[25] As he awaits his father's death, dramatized memory scenes mingle with imaginary episodes in which he projects his relatives into unpleasant situations. As a picaresque radio play "I'm Off Now" is competently written, but limited by its similarity in conception to Keith Waterhouse and Willis Hall's *Billy Liar* (1960). In England, Bland's success as an actor was immediate, and his dramatic output was consequently reduced.

VII *Graham Billing*

For numerous New Zealand writers of the 1960s drama seems to have been a secondary interest in a career devoted mainly to other genres, and their dramatic achievement has probably been restricted by their diversification. Writers like Bland, Baxter, Curnow, and Campbell have written notable plays in spite of the limited nature of their commitment, but for a number of others drama seems to have been regarded primarily as a commercial activity. Since the early 1960s writers have found it possible to supplement their royalties considerably by dramatizing their own novels and short stories for radio. In almost every case the adaptation is markedly inferior to the original and shows no sign of any attempt to conceive the work afresh in dramatic terms; often a narrator is used extensively, with viable dialogue being treated as drama.

The only adaptation of any distinction in this period is Graham Billing's "Forbush and the Penguins," based on his own novel of the same title. In the novel Forbush is left alone in a historic hut in McMurdo Sound for the whole penguin breeding period; his purpose is to make biological observations, and the novel simply follows his attempts to cope with what appear to be quite normal problems in that environment. The structure of the novel is basically rather like that of a diary, but in the radio play much less attention is paid to chronology, the emphasis being placed on Forbush's mental turmoil. A variety of narration is achieved by Forbush speaking to himself, with the use of a letter style and a reading style, and some of this is taken straight from the novel. But the use of extra voices is completely new: the Sun, a Sea Leopard, Mount Erebus, the Ghost of Scott, and a large number of environmental factors are all given voices, creating a continual dialogue inside Forbush. By exploiting the absence of a spatial dimension in radio, Billing was able to construct a drama of one man populating his solitude, similar in principle to Baxter's *Jack Winter's Dream*. A radio version of Billing's *The Slipway* in 1977 had a more conventionally social resonance.

Within four months of the acceptance of "Forbush and the Penguins" in 1965, Billing submitted "Mervyn Gridfern Versus the Baboons," an original play for radio. The play is a fusion of realism and fantasy which emerges from the character of Sullivan who lives with a girl called Susan. As he makes a wardrobe, Sullivan starts telling Susan about Gridfern, a fantasy character of his own, and for the rest of the play their dialogue is interspersed with short dramatized Gridfern episodes. Gridfern takes a pig home from the zoo where he works, and eventually kills and buries it; he goes to the zoo at night, accidentally lets the baboons out, and, after recapturing two of them, shoots a female baboon at the top of a tree. The play ends with the sounds of the baboon's body falling through foliage and hitting the ground. By this stage Sullivan has himself taken over the part of Gridfern, but his relationship with Susan has been so well developed that her absence at the end gives the play an engrossing ambivalence;

although there is nothing explicit to support the notion, the audience has been manipulated into wanting to equate Susan with the female baboon.

The fusion of reality and fantasy in "Mervyn Gridfern Versus the Baboons" could only be achieved on radio, with its potential for suggestion and vagueness of definition. Again, it is a drama of one man's method of populating his inner life, but the motivation of both Sullivan and Gridfern is so confused that the zookeeper sometimes appears as an alter ego. Gridfern is a powerful subconscious figure, and the pig episode seems particularly irrational; however, in spite of this, the dramatic coherence of the piece is faultless, and its tone of sinister absurdity is unique within New Zealand drama.

VIII   *Julian Dickon*

A factor that probably accounts for the unstable output of many radio dramatists is the varying requirements of the New Zealand Broadcasting Corporation, the successor to the New Zealand Broadcasting Service, which in turn evolved into Radio New Zealand in 1975; whatever the nomenclature, all radio drama of any significance has always been produced by a single state-controlled organization. In the early 1960s a shortage of material meant that a high proportion of work submitted was produced, but by the middle of the decade the Corporation was buying about one New Zealand play every week and an unprecedented problem of programming had arisen. Apart from very light material that was used for commercial stations, plays were selected for production to a general audience on the popular "YA" stations or to a more serious audience on the more cultural "YC" stations. It was found that almost all of the better playwrights preferred to write "YC" material, and a continuous attempt was made to encourage such writers to work for a wider audience. Some dramatists, like John Dunmore, Nancy Krinkel, David Yerex, Arthur E. Jones, James Borrows, Alan Trussell-Cullen, and Ivan De La Chaumette, supplied substantial amounts of competently written radio entertainment, often of a detective or historical nature, but the Corporation's greatest success in developing a professional "YA" writer was in the case of Julian Dickon.

From 1964 to 1966 some of Dickon's work showed close affinities with that of Mark Richards especially a tendency toward poetical expression in the treatment of a naïve story-line. But at the same time he was developing the skills of naturalistic drama, most successfully within a rural or nautical context, and in 1967 he wrote "Brindle," a play about a prison escapee and a forestry gang; "Brindle" may be seen as the prototype of "Pukemanu," a highly popular television series which Dickon conceived in 1970, though he retired from the script-writing after disagreements over the first three episodes.

Reviewing Dickon's "Cannibal Rat" in 1970, Eric Bradwell noted "a considerable improvement in the quality of his dialogue," and found "a Pinteresque quality of menace and suspense."[26] Menace and suspense are elements that Dickon continued to exploit, notably in "A House Full of Shadows" (1971), but full-time radio writing led to a search for variety that largely deprived his work of personal characteristics, with a tendency toward sentimentality (especially in endings) and the overworking of a limited number of radio techniques, especially flashbacks. In 1973 a radio reviewer commented that "If Mr. Dickon has a weakness, it is a tendency in difficult dramatic moments to lapse into pretentiousness, or a slight coyness,"[27] and a few months previously Peter Cape has suggested that Dickon's basic problem was "a shortage of stereotypes."[28] Dickon's successors in the "Pukemanu" series amply demonstrated Cape's contention.

After the initial purchase, radio plays generally offer little additional income for the dramatist, who must be continually working at new material. For Julian Dickon, professional radio writing seems to have destroyed his interest in experimentation and to have developed writing habits that might have been eliminated under less pressure.

CHAPTER 8

The Gulbenkian Experiment

TOWARD the end of 1969 Downstage Theatre presented the Gulbenkian Series of eight New Zealand plays, almost all of which were stage premieres; the series included Somerville's "One Man Goon," Dibble's *Lines to M* and "Lord, Dismiss Us . . . ," and Campbell's *When the Bough Breaks*. A grant of seven hundred and fifty pounds was received, somewhat unexpectedly, from the Calouste Gulbenkian Foundation; this was to be used to encourage new theater writers, and Downstage mounted the plays as Sunday night workshop productions between September 1969 and March 1970. The Gulbenkian season was not in any sense a precise turning point in the history of New Zealand drama, but it did epitomize certain developments that were to reach a fruition in the early 1970s.

Since its foundation in 1964 Downstage Theatre had always been an intimate theater, but the Gulbenkian productions introduced audiences to a new order of intimacy. Partly because of limited resources and low budgets, the plays were all mounted with either a minimal set or a compatible set from another production; this meant that the confrontation between actor and audience was almost entirely on a personal basis, unqualified by any decorative element other than the nonrepresentational effects of light and music. This production style epitomized a general trend even in New Zealand suburban theater away from the proscenium and the raised stage, toward intimate production, often in the round. Inevitably, dramatists began writing consciously to exploit these conditions, and the convergence of radio and stage techniques already observed in the Gulbenkian plays of Campbell and Dibble was a stylistic trait of several young writers who came to prominence during and after the series.

I Max B. Richards

Although the inclusion of "The Messengers" in the Gulbenkian season marked the first professional production of a play by Max B. Richards, his work had become widely known through amateur productions in the previous two years. Since 1966 Richards had been an increasingly prolific writer of serious short plays, the characteristics of which were well summarized by Jack Shallcrass: "All his writings explore particular incidents or emotions, the despair and loneliness of old age, boredom, sex without commitment, the corruption of power over persons . . . . His big need is to learn the tricks of making human situations theatrical and dramatic."[1] That Richards's concern for severe economy and simplicity was new to New Zealand drama is confirmed by the critical response, particularly that of Ronald Barker, a man of very considerable experience in theater administration, who stated that a double bill of Richards's plays constituted "two of the finest plays [he had] seen from any New Zealand author." But while *New Zealand Theatre* was hailing Richards as "At Last a Young New Zealand Dramatist!!!"[2] student productions of his plays were being treated unsympathetically at British Drama League festivals.

Innovative as they seemed at the time, a reading of Richards's earliest plays confirms Shallcrass's opinion of their limitations. *The Queue*, regarded by Richards as the best of his early works,[3] involves a group of people waiting to buy tickets. The reason they are waiting is a sign telling them to do so, and their dialogue simply reveals the various expectations that it arouses; at the end of the play, they are still waiting. In *The Roof* four old people sit on the roof of an apartment building; their dialogue establishes that their life is purposeless, and at the end of the play they jump off the roof (upstage). The ending of *The Roof* is an extravagant gesture for Richards; almost all of his earlier plays simply present a static situation sustained for one-act duration by high-quality naturalistic dialogue which occasionally explodes only to subside again.

Reviewing "The Messengers" at Downstage Theatre, Ian Fraser emphasized Richards's debt to Harold Pinter, and pointed out that the play "is little more than a bagatelle, without 'insidious intent,' which comes close to being overwritten."[4] Although the main characters in "The Messengers" do not do very much except talk, they are dramatically more dynamic than most of Richards's early characters because, as killers, they at least have the potential for action. For its Australian premiere in 1972 the play was substantially rewritten and retitled "Mirrors," with the emphasis more deliberately on the vein of black comedy. The setting is a hall of mirrors in a deserted funfair, where two gunmen are waiting beside their bound victim; one is a middle-aged veteran, the other is an acned twenty-two-year-old on his first job, and much of the comedy comes from their divergent attitudes to the imminent killing. At the play's comic crisis, the apprentice "messenger" announces that he has arranged to meet a girl at the fair "after work," and from that point the mood darkens until the final episode, in which the senior killer knifes his partner and then turns on the girl and the victim. Although the dialogue generates a realistic intensity with its local phrasing and New Zealand references, this is counterpointed visually by the distorting mirrors which reflect all the action. In different ways all the speaking characters—like the audience—are in learning situations, but the instrument of that learning is patently unreliable; much of the decisive action is played upstage into the mirrors, and at the end the girl's recognition of her killer is surrounded by bizarre reflections. A similar truncation of action occurs in Richards's *Sadie and Neco* (1968), in which the central characters talk about themselves in the third person and the apparent hypochondria of one of them is subjected to a grotesque exercise in voyeurism.

By the time the Gulbenkian Series was produced, Richards had been appointed resident playwright to the new Mercury Theatre in Auckland; with a seating capacity of over six hundred, it is by far the largest professional theater in New Zealand and was wholly unsuitable for Richards's work. Consequently, in 1970 he began to concentrate on radio drama. "Engaged" consists of a dialogue between a newly engaged couple at a bus stop, and "Cinderella Jones" is almost entirely dialogue between an unmarried couple in and around a car, with a brief appearance by the woman's husband; "Why Don't We Call Him Zarathustra" is a conversation between a young couple expecting their first child, and "Threshold" involves a family group having an engagement party. While resident at the Mercury Theatre, Richards wrote several other similar radio plays and some short stage pieces, none of which was formally staged; he then went overseas, and some of his later work, like *Cripple Play* (1973), has been produced in Australia and London as well as, belatedly, in New Zealand.

In his New Zealand work Richards never learned the "tricks of making human situations theatrical," the most significant defect that Shallcrass found in his early work. His drama emerges from an interesting premise, a concept of complete parity between character and audience which is very much in accordance with the Downstage ideal of intimacy: in almost every play, he simply sets up a sign or a situation which calls for a reaction, and allows his characters and his audience to explore the scope for reaction together. Because of the minimal exposition and deliberately shallow characterization, the work has to be sustained by a prospective atmosphere. In *The Queue* (as in several of his early plays) the characters are not named or even given much differentiation, and the exposition consists just of a sign "CIRCUS. PLEASE QUEUE."[5] The whole drama is precipitated by the sign, and once the mystery of the sign loses interest the drama collapses. But when the initial situation is itself devoid of mystery, as in most of his radio plays, the drama is never able to generate a prospective atmosphere and the play seems inconsequential from the start.

The refinement of Richards's drama has occurred within the context of Australian drama largely because of an astonishing lack of strategy in the national coordination of emergent professional theater: neither Richards nor the Mercury Theatre had any real use for each other.

II   *Owen Leeming*

"The Quarry Game," Owen Leeming's contribution to the Gulbenkian Series, illustrates the difficulties in extending the premises of Max Richards into full-length work. Like all of Leeming's stage plays, "The Quarry Game" calls for no set and minimal properties; as each character enters, he asks what the location is, and is told it is a quarry. As in Richards's plays, the characters and the audience start from a similar level of ignorance, and it seems that the main activity is to consist of waiting for another character, called Lom. Also, there is some uncertainty about the type of characterization Leeming is using; the characters are mostly unnamed, their relationship is very vague even to themselves, and a peculiar ageing process seems to be operating on them, so that the atmosphere is prospective, with an edge of science fiction. At this point, a metatheatrical cliché is introduced in the form of two more characters posing as audience members trying to get out; the actors ostensibly stop the play (although they do not come out of their roles) and conduct a lengthy argument with the "audience" about their reasons for leaving. As a theater piece, the play fails to recover from this cliché, but Leeming's subsequent treatment of it is interesting; the two "audience" members fully accept the existence of the quarry, and they seem to be absorbed into the same vague relationships and ageing process as the actors, a process which turns out to be most advanced in Lom. By the end of the play, the man and woman from the audience are apparently in their own living room; they have taken the play home with them and are left frozen in a state of advanced age.

The principle of parity between actors and audience observed in the work of Richards thus reaches more elaborate dimensions in "The Quarry Game." But the virtual elimination of character, spectacle, and action places an emphasis on style which the play, with its heavy echoes of Beckett and its clumsy exploitation of the theatrical situation, cannot possibly sustain. Nor was Leeming's problem entirely a matter of duration: a much shorter play, "Four," experiments with a theatrical situation that leaves the "play" behind in a much cruder fashion, and "Ex" simply presents two people talking at cross purposes, with a few sharply defined character changes.

Before the Gulbenkian Series, Leeming's dramatic experience had been mainly in the directing of radio and television plays, and when he began writing radio plays in 1969 he immediately showed a technical versatility which was not matched by his narrative skills. "Order" (1969) is a study of an old military man and of the family relationships that his career has fostered; food preparation is treated with the same finesse as battle strategy, and kitchen scenes merge with memories of Africa, both supplied by the Describer who presides over the play. "Yellow" (1969) is essentially a dialogue between a New Zealand soldier in Vietnam and his brain, the whole play being a fifty-minute expansion of about the last minute before his death. The mechanics of the play are very complex; memory is dramatized through a number of minor characters, as is his speculation about how others would react to the same situation, and several neutral voices supply knowledge and statistical information. "Yellow" was followed by "Reefer's Boys" (1970), a simple historical drama about a gang during the Depression; it is stylistically unambitious, but its narrative development is considerably more cohesive than in any of Leeming's earlier plays.

In most of the radio and stage plays of both Richards and Leeming, disregard for conventional exposition and story development gives an impression of shapelessness which makes extraordinary demands on whatever continuity devices they use. Both writers often seem concerned to create the impression that the dramatic situation has escaped authorial control so that actors and audience may explore a situation together. Richards has said that *The Queue* developed from an exercise in improvisation,[6] and much of his other work suggests a similar origin. Leeming's use of the Describer in "Order," the neutral voices of the Computer and the Control Girl in "Yellow," and his determination to call a stage a stage in his theater work all seem primarily an attempt at objectivity. But the result for both of them is generally a focus on style which neither can sustain for any duration.

III   *Edward Bowman*

Some of the general problems of Richards and Leeming were solved in Edward Bowman's play, *Salve Regina*, which in 1969 received its first productions on radio, television, and stage; in different forms, the New Zealand Broadcasting Corporation produced it in March, London Weekend Television in May, and Downstage Theatre in the Gulbenkian Series in September. For each production (including the first), Bowman rewrote the script incorporating and adapting details from the other media, and although the published script[7] represents the television version it includes details that were added when Bowman was thinking of the work in radio terms.

The television and stage versions of *Salve Regina* are set in the basement of a department store which has apparently been wrecked in a nuclear war, although the reliability of the characters is always in doubt. Time and location have become meaningless, although, again, the audience is uncertain whether the destruction of the rest of the world is a dramatic reality, a pretense by the characters, or a combination of both. Moreover, there is a deliberate confusion of period: the men have adopted *commedia dell'arte* names, Pulchinella and Arlecchino, and the woman is simply called "the Queen." Their dialogue is constructed as "a cross between the formality of the heads of state talking to each other," and "a sort of basic vulgarity,"[8] and the character relationships are heavily ritualized from the start.

The context at the opening of the play thus contains an element of mystery, but the characterization is deliberately shallow. The three characters are in the process of becoming dehumanized; their building is surrounded by starving dogs, and survival is forcing the characters themselves to become more animal. Bowman's drama is consequently poised on an evolutionary factor such as Leeming used in "The Quarry Game," when a new character is introduced, and the whole situation is suddenly charged with a new vitality. The Queen has sterilized herself, and her relationship with the men is on an extremely crude level. But the newcomer, Marina Patek, is an attractive young virgin, and the audience immediately relates to her as a fragile, sympathetic, human element in an animal context; within the play, there is also the possibility that Arlecchino and Pulchinella will show a similar response and the evolutionary process will be neutralized. The ambivalence of this situation is explored in the central part of the play, and reaches a climax when the Queen challenges Marina's capacity to rear a child, and is herself annihilated; but although the episode ostensibly presents the triumph of Marina over the Queen, the fact that she herself is reduced to animal level in the process means that the evolutionary issue is as ambivalent as before. In the final episode Marina makes a last defiant gesture toward the men but then succumbs to survival on their terms, whatever that may imply.

Salve Regina thus begins and ends with a chaotic, subhuman situation, and its dramatic coherence comes from the attempt to find order in that chaos, an attempt which is invested largely in the characters of Marina and the Queen. Ostensibly, it is Marina who offers the possibility of order, since she alone appears to be governed by motives other than sex and survival, but the suggestion of logic in the Queen's assumption of her role is not found in the work of Leeming and Richards and itself constitutes a shaping factor in the drama; it means that, as the drama of relationships develops thematic solidity, there is also an evaluation of roles which allows a dramatic resolution. However, Bowman's main concern is with the function rather than the origin of roles, and it seems immaterial to him that his characters emerge from such stereotyped situations: that Marina tumbles down from outer space to land just beside the three other survivors must indicate direct contempt for plausibility of exposition, and yet that element has been vigorously attacked by numerous critics.[9]

Possibly to acknowledge blatantly the contrived nature of Marina's arrival, in the radio script Bowman used a narrator and included several brief episodes of Marina in a space vehicle approaching Earth; even the landing is dramatized. The presence of the narrator, who was also used in the Gulbenkian stage version, dispels any suggestion of a realistic atmosphere. Also, there is a further degree of stylization in the locations implied in the radio version: space is equated with heaven, Earth with limbo, and the hole where the Queen dies is hell. Bowman derived the idea from a morality play, and it accords well with the general pattern of the action.

Bowman's achievement in *Salve Regina* is difficult to assess, largely because of the number of versions and the changes made by each director due to production conditions. The television version was placed first out of nearly three thousand entries in the 1968 London *Observer* playwriting competition after a very mixed response by the judges: it was "strongly defended by [Harold] Pinter, and strongly attacked by [Kenneth] Tynan, although he conceded it would work on stage."[10] Pinter was expected to direct the television production, although he expressed reservations about the play's use of rhetoric, reservations which are supported by an examination of Bowman's other work; the central strength of all his plays lies in their vigorous and audacious dramatic conception, but their basic literary quality is not always sufficient to support them if the dramatic vigor lapses.

The clearest example of Bowman's dramatic enterprise exceeding his literary ability is in the radio play "Solus" (1973). None of Bowman's plays has more than one character who is fully humanized, but in "Solus" the situation is accentuated, with the whole drama focusing on the sole survivor of the human race who is caught up in intergalactic warfare among futuristic automata. The play has humorous elements, but its development can only involve man's resignation to a mechanized universe. As in *Salve Regina*, Bowman's preoccupation with the function of each component in a necessarily balanced situation gives a degree of dramatic shape, but the computerized language soon loses its interest.

Two of Bowman's other works have been produced on stage and radio under the collective title of "Questions of Loyalty," but they were written quite separately and intended for different media, although, as exercises in monologue writing, adaptation was relatively simple. *John* is a brief work, constructed around a single revelation at the end: that the woman who is painting her husband's portrait has left the rest of his body outside. The final equation of the husband with John the Baptist makes the whole play a simple but effective dramatic conceit, exploiting radio in the same way as Dibble had done in "A Recital."

"Iscariot" was originally written as a sketch for a much longer television play. Judas Iscariot is trapped in a German brothel which literally echoes with Nazi atrocities; his monologue consists mainly of self-defense against his reputation as an archetypal traitor. The language of the play is somewhat reminiscent of *Salve Regina* in the way that it uses New Testament texts as a basis for stylization, and the element of tension between characters—noticeably lacking in "Solus"—is skillfully exploited here. Iscariot's reliability is continuously in doubt, but the way his dialectic is placed against New Testament narrative manipulates the audience's prejudices and sympathies into an ultimately inconclusive situation; since Judas has never been allowed a hearing like this before, an element of compensation is established early, and this is consolidated by references to the persecution of Jews at Auschwitz. The stage version ends with Judas stabbing the brothel keeper, conflagration noises, a slide of corpses, and Judas leaving the stage, screaming about "Godless Religion."

The fusion of two historical situations, both of which invite debate on the issue of responsibility, means that the work as a whole is something of an exercise in dramatic ambiguity; one does not know whether the example of Judas serves as a prototype for Nazi behavior, or whether his own dramatized sadism is simply a product of German conditioning. All of Bowman's plays take the audiences to the frenetic fringes of humanity, but in "Iscariot" the audience is caught between two such extremes, and the substantially different structuring of the same components in each version emphasizes that the basic impact of the play is one of intimidation and that details of dramatic shape are secondary to the grossness of the material. Among other important dramatic idiosyncrasies, Bowman stands out among New Zealand playwrights for his determinedly Artaudian propensities.

IV *Anthony Taylor*

Both the radio and stage versions of *Salve Regina* were first directed by Anthony Taylor, who was then a prominent radio producer and in 1976 was appointed artistic director of Downstage Theatre. Taylor's production style has had a noticeable influence on the work of several younger playwrights, and he himself is the author of several plays for stage and radio. The first of these, "Wherever You Are" (1968), is a portrait of a weak-willed, weak-minded boy who is dislocated from society, scared of close human contact, and sheltered by fantasies, which he apparently conceives as realities. As the boy drifts through life in a small town, he composes letters in his mind, explaining what he is doing and what has happened to him; the letter motif and the characterization of the boy give continuity to the play. However, almost at the end the action shifts to the Post Office Dead Letter Department, where two mail sorters casually refer to an accumulation of letters addressed only to "You, Wherever You Are." The play thus ends with the abrupt dramatic annihilation of the fantasy, though without harming the boy, who happily sets off down the road to another town. The boy's role is shattered, but his character is intact, and the structural finality of the ending comes in the revelation that what has been presented as studied, formal communication is in fact complete noncommunication.

"Wherever You Are" was based on one of Taylor's short stories, but most of his other work has been written specifically as radio drama and involves variations on an interview situation. "There Is No Story" (1969) is presided over by an Announcer, who listens to a Man's narrative of a recent love relationship, occasionally asking very general questions; the atmosphere of the play is suggestive of a formal interrogation, although the Announcer's precise role is never defined. "Any Questions" (1972) involves two men who have developed a nightly ritual of questioning, apparently without any purpose, though with a domestic emphasis. A woman comes in, ridicules their ritual, suggests they are homosexuals, and departs; alone, the men return to their ritual, their relationship, which is obviously consolidated by the questioning, having been further stimulated by the woman's intrusion.

Digby (1972) involves a simple man going through three formal interviews, apparently for marriage guidance purposes, though this is only vaguely implicit. Between the interviews he has conversations with his wife and with a homosexual whom he lives with. Digby is very much like an adult version of the boy in "Wherever You Are"; he is slow-witted, inarticulate, unable to understand what people expect of him, and at the end of the play he is quite happily left on his own, supported as a character by his dauntless stupidity and naïve honesty, but left without a role now that the interviews are over.

Taylor's basic approach to radio drama is that characters "exist inside their own minds; they don't have to have exteriors." This he expands: "There Is No Story" again to me is a person locked inside his own mind. He had to be activated by something. He wouldn't of his own volition spill it all out. It was important to me that the Announcer was just the Announcer, that he should in no way ever assume any other characteristics, of a psychiatrist or detective, or anything like that . . . . I don't know who the Announcer is, I don't know what he's doing; he's simply the catalyst from which the memory must spring."[11] This concept of a dramatic catalyst makes available a very wide range of characters. It is one of the unspoken premises of *When the Bough Breaks, Lines to M, John,* and numerous similar plays that the central characters have a need to express their memories or fantasies. Taylor's characters are dependent on no such need, and so they are in no way vulnerable to the effects of the dramatic action; whether an announcer, a letter, or an interviewer, the catalyst is of purely mechanical significance.

There is an obvious similarity between Taylor's use of a dramatic catalyst and the functional approach to character observed in the work of Edward Bowman; the relationship between character and catalyst involves the kind of tentative role creation found in *Salve Regina,* and "Solus" exposes a single human to a wholly mechanical environment. However, the reduction of a character to the level of a pure dramatic function raises an issue of language which Bowman had carried to its extreme in "Solus," to the complete detriment of the play. Taylor's Interviewer in *Digby* operates in a way that is almost as mechanical as the futuristic figures in "Solus," but there is an important difference in their potential effects: even the Interviewer's first question implies the existence of a social context that may possibly accommodate Digby, and there is always the dramatic possibility that Taylor's characters may outgrow their roles and the whole interview situation.

Two of Taylor's short plays received stage premieres at Downstage Theatre in 1978. In "Sweet Israel," "a duet for middle age," a couple indulges in sterile, inert introversion; the man questions himself about the possibility of relationships, and the woman speaks to herself about the world crisis, particularly about the war in the Middle East. The action covers a day: breakfast at home, lunch in a restaurant, afternoon coffee (separately), and dinner together. From time to time they articulate their concerns in an attempt at conversation. These characters are relatively self-aware, but their final stance simply vindicates solipsism, with the two lines of theme development resolving into a very satisfying formal harmony at the end.

Taylor's plays sometimes achieve a remarkable level of abstraction, comparable with that of the Pinter plays of the late 1960s; when, as in "Sweet Israel," there is a parity of expressive energy between the characters, the texture of the dialogue may be tightly resolved in terms of form but totally open-ended on a thematic level. However, in "The Odds against Evan" Taylor reverted to more specifically individualized characterization and a cast of seven to portray a day with a young would-be painter; a cumulative line of religious imagery results in an awkward and bizarre ending, in which Evan crucifies a young friend as a model for a painting. The play confirms the opinion that Taylor's strength and originality is in the severely economical treatment of generic material.

V *Robert Lord*

The most sustained attempt to translate principles like Taylor's into stage terms has been in the work of Robert Lord, who was at Downstage Theatre at the time of the Gulbenkian Series but whose first play was not produced until 1971. Taylor has been responsible for the radio and stage production of most of Lord's best work, and some plays, like "Well Hung" (1974), were revised in association with Taylor during rehearsals. However, Lord appears to have written his first play, *It Isn't Cricket* (1971), quite independently, and his working relationship with Taylor seems to have been essentially a partnership between a writer and a director with remarkably similar dramatic principles.

The introductory directions to *It Isn't Cricket* indicate the extremely economical nature of Lord's early work:

> No description of the characters is given here apart from the obvious fact that Viv and Kath are women and the others men. The ages of the characters are not important, except that they are all of the one generation. While there is a chronological sequence in the eighteen scenes in this play the passage of time has not been indicated outside the text because it has no relevance . . . . I would suggest that the play be staged on a single and minimal set which would allow fluidity (I think the quick juxtaposition of scenes is essential) and suggest that the location along with the chronology has no relevance.[12]

Each scene is presented as a dialogue on a defined topic, generally with a simple stichomythian pattern which establishes a basic rhythm, and the scene titles suggest ritual confrontation between characters:

SCENE ONE Viv and Jason at home.
SCENE TWO Jason and Paul discuss cricket.
SCENE THREE Viv and Paul talk about cricket.
SCENE FOUR Viv, Jason and Paul play canasta.
SCENE FIVE Jason and Viv talk about her career.
SCENE SIX Paul and Jason talk about Viv and her career . . . . [13]

In each scene the discussion topic offers a dramatic catalyst. The characters are established within a context of games, and other topics are introduced so that they appear as game situations; the rules which govern their games are extended to cover the rest of their lives, and form a basis for character evaluation. Gradually, lying and cheating become the dominant issues, and the play reaches its climax in the sixteenth scene, when Paul is proven to be a liar.

It Isn't Cricket is much too long to be sustained by such a slight development in the characters' relationships, and the introduction of three more characters in the last two acts is hard to justify. Neither of these objections, however, could apply to Lord's next play, "Friendship Centre" (1971), which presents a very similar situation in a much more compact manner: four characters have a dinner party and eventually arrive at a moment of truth. However, there is a persistent vagueness about what constitutes "truth," and the lives of the characters outside the dinner party situation are indicated only in generic terms; they talk about "the islands," "the natives," and "the war," and there is a strongly implied contrast between their superficial relationships and a mysterious "Friendship Centre" down the road. In spite of the better cohesion of this script, in neither the radio production of 1972 nor the television version of 1973 was the enigmatically generic nature of their environment sufficiently apparent to establish any real atmosphere.

Lord's major play in this early style is *Meeting Place* (1972), which again presents two men and two women moving through a pattern of relationships; the location is not defined, and in this play Lord abandons all suggestions of chronological structure. In Taylor's production at Downstage Theatre the whole action was performed on two bare rostra, with any trace of realism being broken by aggressive lighting.

At the start of *Meeting Place* the four actors are engaged in separate monologues, all concerned with vague memories of meetings with strangers, and none of them apparently aware of the others' memories. Nothing in the first scene indicates any relationship among the speakers, or even establishes their identity as characters; the effect of the scene is to create grounds for a communal memory among the characters and the audience. The central action presents the actors in character (though only very tenuously related to the "communal memory" at the start), moving together in a series of heterosexual and homosexual relationships; most of the play involves dialogue similar to that of Lord's earlier work, but for the first time the script includes simple actions such as kisses, fights, and a rape. By the end of the play the characters have formed homosexual couples, and their actions include elements of the "communal memory" before they retire into monologues on the theme of solitude.

Meeting Place is thus dramatically ambiguous in a way similar to Taylor's "There Is No Story," in which the man being interrogated continually doubts his own memory. But in *Meeting Place* the deliberate confusion of chronology, especially between the monologues and the rest of the action, means that there is an ultimate uncertainty as to the direction in which memory is operating; equally viable interpretations involve regarding the central action as dramatized memory or as dramatized thought-projection, both viewed from the perspective of the monologues. The return to monologue at the end makes this ambiguity inescapable, and so, although either the monologues or the central action must involve telepathic projection, the process is not allowed to crystallize in such a way as to make it mechanically obtrusive, as had happened in Bradwell's "The Last Station."

Meeting Place is artistically Lord's most ambitious and successful work, exploring its abstract subject within a technique that skillfully exploits the already observed tendency toward a generic vision. But in terms of general theatrical effectiveness it is limited by a lack of narrative interest at the start; the production was not a commercial success at Downstage Theatre, even though it was mounted at a time when stage nudity was still very much a novelty.

Although it was only after *Meeting Place* that Lord noticeably began shaping his work toward public taste, he had shown a propensity toward comedy in two other works written in 1972. "Moody Tuesday," his first play written specifically for radio, again centers around two men and two women, very like the bourgeois stereotypes in "Friendship Centre." Lord described the play at the time of its first presentation: "The banality of the plot reflects its derivation—the world of popular fiction. The concern of the play is not so much with the plot as with the characters whose lives have been moulded into stereotypes by the fictions about the reality that they now appear in. It is the morality of this two-dimensional world that is important. "Moody Tuesday" is an egocentric's play. The people don't really listen to each other or think about what they are saying. They and their reactions to any given situation are fixed in the fictions they emulate."[14]

As in *Meeting Place*, the conception of the whole play suggests the extension of Taylor's interview situation to involve four people; whereas Taylor's basic method examines one person "locked inside his mind," Lord presents four egocentrics. The need for a catalyst is solved in *Meeting Place* by the communal memory, and in this play Lord finds a similar function for "plot," a novelty in his plays to this point, and here largely personalized in the form of a blackmailer. The four central characters think and act in the terms of a love comic; much of the action is devoted to their thought sequences, and in Taylor's radio production it was intentionally difficult to determine the level of realism. The play ends with the ease of a popular romance, without any apparent serious implications; its comedy emerges from the way it epitomizes a certain type of behavior uncritically. In "Moody Tuesday" the catalyst is used for illustration rather than for analysis, and the result is inevitably superficial.

While *Meeting Place* was running at Downstage Theatre, a shorter play of Lord's was produced at Unity Theatre. *Balance of Payments* was completed after *Meeting Place*, but Lord had been working on it intermittently for several years, and the obvious influence of Edward Albee (which is not noticeable in any of Lord's other work) suggests that its origins might have come from his first association with Downstage, in a production of *A Delicate Balance* in 1968. *Balance of Payments* is a black comedy, a portrait of a sterile society with a curiously perverted system of values; it involves a middle-aged couple who are apparently supported by their son, a prostitute, but they nevertheless treat the situation—along with every trivial detail in their lives—with a meticulous sense of propriety. In production, the play was the most popular of Lord's early work, especially because of its farcical ending, but its main critical interest lies in its language; in his use of repetitious, hackneyed, overexplicit dialogue which deliberately subverts normal speech rhythms, Lord found a comic style that he continued to use in most of his subsequent work. However, his attempts to apply it to basically serious themes have resulted in a general confusion of intentions, especially apparent in a series of four police dramas written in 1973.

"The Body in the Park" was Lord's second play written for radio, and seems very similar in conception to "Moody Tuesday." It begins in a police station where two detectives are engaged in reading an Agatha Christie novel; they discuss it intermittently throughout the play, briefly applying their attention to their own work, which they analyze in the terms of a popular thriller. Most of the play is successful farce with a slight satirical undertone, but at the end it suddenly becomes very serious; a young policeman, frustrated with the methods of his colleagues, hangs himself in a police lavatory. In "Moody Tuesday" Lord made no attempt to question the validity of his comic material; in "The Body in the Park" he does so, but without a realistic context for that evaluation his attempt seems clumsy and incongruous.

"Blood on My Sprigs" was written at about the same time as "The Body in the Park" and was also intended for radio. The beginning is reminiscent of Lord's early work: two men and two women are living in adjacent cottages, and the action is precipitated by the more virile of the men shifting in with one of the women. The other man, a latent homosexual, is not much concerned, and simply gets another companion; however, the single woman, Lydia, is so upset that she hangs herself with the laces from one of the men's rugby boots. This brings Sergeant Morrisey to the scene, but the play ends with the "case" unresolved and the domestic relationships of all the characters very much in doubt.

In its construction "Blood on My Sprigs" is much more complex than can be suggested in summary, and represents an attempt to fuse the style of Lord's plays about domestic relationships with that of those based on popular fiction. Sergeant Morrisey is a character who also occurs in "The Body in the Park." and he appears in "Blood on My Sprigs" in a very similar role; Lydia spends most of her evenings reading or listening to stories about Detective Morrisey of the Mounted Police, and the materialization of the same figure after her death retrospectively throws doubt on the whole play's basis in realism. In an indeterminate way, there is a factor of communal thought projection such as was suggested in *Meeting Place;* but because this factor is apparent only after the hanging, the play manages to question the validity of popular stereotypes from the perspective of established realistic values.

A dramaturgic problem arises about what to do with such values after they have been established and exploited. In "Blood on My Sprigs" Lord attempts to consolidate them by crippling another young man in a car accident in which Morrisey is not involved, and fading the play out with the domestic consequences of the main action and another installment of the activities of the Detective. But when he revised the same material for a stage play, "I'll Scream if I Want To," Lord wrote eight additional domestic scenes which he placed at the beginning and end of the play, and adapted the ending of every scene to involve a verbal formula about whether the characters really "care" about what happens. Morrisey is a character who conspicuously does not "care," and the total impact of the theme is a general statement about the difference between personal and public relationships; however, the formulaic endings appear as a self-conscious coherence devicé and the extra scenes remain unjustified.

Lord's best-known and most controversial police drama is "Well Hung," which premiered at Downstage Theatre in January 1974. "Well Hung" is an extensively revised version of "The Body in the Park," and it also culminates with a young policeman, disgusted and frustrated, hanging himself in a police station. However, instead of using crime fiction as the determinant of police methods, in "Well Hung" Lord develops a naturalistic New Zealand atmosphere which gradually establishes an implicit documentary basis; most of the play's early critics recognized that the central action was drawn from the Crewe murder case,[15] and in Taylor's production the documentary sources were emphasized by the use of newspaper facsimiles for the program and for the set. Bruce Mason pointed out the parallels in detail: "In the second act, the farce takes a violent slew to the black. A local suspect, accused of amatory interest in the wife of the murdered pair, is introduced, cowed by [Detective] Smart, then beaten into submissive pulp by Bert. At first protesting complete innocence, he finally confesses in the very words attributed to Arthur Allan Thomas, 'All right, if you say so.' He is then shot on the spot by Bert . . . . [Smart] retires in satisfaction to his office, to be slightly fazed by a hanging body: Bert's. Hence the title . . . ."[16]

The pattern of audience manipulation in "Well Hung" becomes very starkly exposed. The whole action occurs in the police station, and starts with a young constable trying to sell his car and arrange for an illegal abortion before he begins his official day's work. The early episodes are developed with such realistic skill that the implications about police corruption are suppressed by the comedy, and, as parallels with specific local murders begin to emerge, so does the play take on a farcical intensity. In this way the audience is thoroughly compromised, but, as in "The Body in the Park," the attempt to revalue the material at the end is awkwardly contrived. The sudden realization of the title has some relevance to police ethics as presented in the play, but none at all to the nonfictional basis, and the change in tone punctures the atmosphere without heightening the implied argument.

Toward the end of 1973 Robert Lord followed Max Richards in being appointed resident playwright to the Mercury Theatre, Auckland; again, a young writer whose stage work had been exclusively concerned with intimate conditions was confronted with a large, traditionally designed theater. Lord's first Auckland work was "Nativity," a crucifixion play which seems primarily an exercise in working with a large cast; it was premiered at Theatre Co-op, Auckland, in December 1973.

For Mercury Theatre a full-length play was commissioned, and Lord's reaction was essentially to extend elements of his established style on to a larger scale. "Heroes and Butterflies" is his most elaborate presentation of a generic world picture; its characters talk about the war, the country, and the rebels, without any indication of the place or period in which the action is located. The themes are largely political, but as well as official and domestic settings some scenes occur in a garden, where a girl is preoccupied with a story that if her cat eats a butterfly it will be poisoned by it; this serves as an obvious parallel to the main action. Richard Campion, who directed the premiere, found that "behind the mocking satire and the nightmarish farce" the play "reveals with delicate precision the changing nature of personality,"[17] a reading which must partially account for the failure of the production; Lord's interest has always been in the areas of relationships between people, and he seems deliberately cursory in his attention to individual personality. For Anthony Taylor's radio production in 1975 Lord subtitled the play "A Child's Garden of Vices," and in Taylor's production at Downstage Theatre in 1978 the typical nature of the material was emphasized by Raymond Boyce's design, incorporating a colossal Winged Victory statue.

In "Friendship Centre" the generic—rather than specific—view of things reflects a group of people who have a need for closeness because the vagueness of their environment makes it seem alien; intimacy among themselves is their only escape, and the establishment of personal closeness offers the possibility of making the generic recede. In "Heroes and Butterflies," on the other hand, intimacy is a political liability, and the characters' official positions make the generalized perspective obligatory. Because of the absence of any sense of closeness, the play is limited in essentially the same way as "Moody Tuesday": a generic vision which compounds the shallowness of personality without positing any other terms for the characters' existence.

Since 1974 Lord has lived in New York, writing for radio and stage in what he terms a "comedy-of-manners" style.[18] New Zealand productions of his work have become less frequent, but he remains an important transitional writer for his sustained attempt to reconcile the intimate reality of most New Zealand theater with the generic and abstract possibilities of a severely economical dramaturgy.

CHAPTER 9

The Confrontational Drama of the 1970s

THOUGH their awareness of contemporary British and American drama was sometimes transparent, the contributors to the Gulbenkian Series still belonged to a pioneer theater, snatching the limited accessible resources and maximizing their dramatic potential. Thus, the actors, poets, radio writers, and novelists of the early 1960s became the playwrights of the final pioneering phase, and in turn mostly yielded to the rise of the specialist playwrights of the 1970s. Pivotal to this development was the consolidation of the new community theaters. As long as Downstage Theatre was virtually alone, its position seemed precarious and its adventurous production policy depended on the patronage of a sympathetic elite. But with the emergence of similar theaters in Auckland, Christchurch, Wanganui, Tauranga, Dunedin, Palmerston North, and Hamilton, presentation of the new drama became more publicly competitive. The new atmosphere permeated the amateur theater as well, but the role of radio in the playwright's education declined as audience confrontation and immediacy of atmosphere became high priorities in the attempt to promote theater as a unique art form. Many of the new playwrights had a background in university drama, and the subtle literary expressionism of earlier writers generally lost favor before more vigorous confrontational techniques developed from theorists like Bertolt Brecht and Jerzy Grotowski.

With the liberation of theatrical styles came a new freedom in articulating local themes. Most of Lord's plays, as well as those of the Gulbenkian writers, were, in effect, located in limbo, an evasion of explicitness which may be related to the factor of national self-consciousness that impeded earlier realistic drama. But the new writers were mostly fearlessly specific, localizing their plays sharply and critically dissecting national institutions, customs, and celebrities. Brian McNeill's *The Two Tigers,* conceived in 1971 and premiered in 1973, is a stage biography of Katherine Mansfield and Middleton Murry which, technically, could belong to the intimate stage of the 1960s, with its minimal set, two named characters, and two multi-role supporting parts. It is a subtle piece which was produced extensively around New Zealand in its first three years, but its opening night was theatrically stunning primarily because a New Zealand saint was exposed, in her consumptive flesh, on the New Zealand stage. Concurrently with *The Two Tigers* at Auckland's Central Theatre, the Mercury Theatre offered its first major production of a New Zealand play, also a biographical study: James McNeish's "The Rocking Cave" is based on the figure of a nineteenth-century religious tyrant in the Waipu area, and needs a large cast and elaborate presentational detail which only the Mercury Theatre could then provide. Two years later McNeish returned to Mercury with "The Mouse Man," a stylized didactic play set in a prison, and "1895," a New Zealand historical play adapted from one of his radio works. In 1979 McNeill wrote a commissioned play for Mercury Theatre, to mark the bicentenary of James Cook's death: "The Naval Officer" is a historical epic conceived to exploit a big theater, stylistically almost the antithesis of *The Two Tigers.* However, illustrative historical drama has commanded less critical attention than plays that strategically question the validity of their local material, an approach which would scarcely have been politic for the Cook anniversary but which might have increased the durability of plays like "The Rocking Cave."

I   *Mervyn Thompson*

As codirector of The Court Theatre, Christchurch, until 1974, and as artistic director of Downstage Theatre from 1975 until his appointment as the head of drama studies at the University of Auckland in 1977, Mervyn Thompson has occupied a uniquely influential position in New Zealand drama in terms of both his production style and his dramaturgic methods. In 1971, the first year of The Court Theatre's existence, he directed Dibble's *Lines to M,* and later did an important revival of Mason's *Awatea,* but his experience in handling large student casts in works like *Marat/Sade* was of considerable importance to the development of his own plays.

First Return, Thompson's first play, was written in 1971 and revised extensively before its premiere at The Court Theatre in 1974, and its revivals have incorporated further revisions. The play's coincidental similarities with Bradwell's *Clay* emphasize the vital importance of expressionism to a culture striving toward self-articulation: the action alternates between realistic scenes located in London and internal scenes in which the protagonist confronts various functions of his own psyche, represented as a "menagerie." Bradwell's clay goblins are parallelled by this group of ten figures dressed in black with traces of "green mould,"[1] and the ending again comes with the psychic chorus rising in a crescendo of demonic laughter, though otherwise the deployment of the menagerie is more in the manner of Frank Wedekind than of Strindberg.

In its thematic complexity, however, *First Return* far transcends the achievement of its expressionistic antecedents in New Zealand drama. Simon, the protagonist, is visiting London, where he meets the only other realistic character, Christine, whose expatriate strangeness functions as a catalyst to the menagerie's aggression. Simon is a character of considerable experience, but his purpose in going to London is to leave that experience behind him; so early in the first act a tension is generated between Simon's chosen role of ingenuous adventurer and Simon's inescapable role as the victim of many facets of New Zealand life. His vestigial New Zealand conditioning, always latent in his mind, is externalized in his menagerie of antipodean types; some of these, like the Father and Mother, are consistently individualized, but most of them, like Authority and Rough, represent generalized social figures who intermittently crystallize into specific roles. Ultimately, all of the menagerie are subsumed by its choric function, so that Simon's isolation is accentuated by his context of collective aggression.

The realistic scenes of *First Return* reflect Simon's failure to find sanctuary in London, and serve mainly to frame the nightmare; at the end of both the second and third acts, the intensity of the hallucination is such that he wakes and staggers into the arms of Christine, but the recurrence of nightmarish motifs like his mother's death in both acts means that exorcism may only be achieved by confronting those motifs on their own territory. The play's theatricality makes greater narrative impact than its dialogue, with much of the haunting atmosphere conceived in terms of performance imagery which is never precisely articulated. But there is also a great deal of incidental naturalistic detail, particularly in episodes of Simon's adolescence.

The loosely autobiographical origin of *First Return* made the expressionistic framing an obvious structure, but in places the hallucinatory content generates an autonomy and bursts outside the frame; this is explicitly scripted in the ending, but the use of folk motifs and antipodean archetypes in the body of the play makes this energy an inevitability in production. In his subsequent works Thompson has dispensed with subjective framing and developed techniques to consolidate the collective eye of the audience, often through building up a sentimental atmosphere heavily edged with irony and thoroughly vulnerable to Brechtian defamiliarization.

O! Temperance!, which premiered under Thompson's direction at The Court Theatre in 1972, is subtitled "a semi-documentary play, with music, on the Temperance Movement in New Zealand to 1919," and generates its basic irony by viewing the historical material from the perspective of the temperance workers themselves; thus, at the end, the characters move among the audience, urging them to sign pledges. Vaudeville and sentimental songs were used incidentally in *First Return*, but here become dominant, and a cartoon-style didacticism is prominent in the presentational methods. However, counterweighting the historical caricature and the use of choric hysteria is a great deal of documentary evidence presented in a heavily localized manner, so that the self-parody of the characters is never unqualified; an American journalist terms the leading prohibitionist "The Savonarola of New Zealand," and the *Tuapeka Times* expands the opinion, but in the next scene the man's obituaries are presented, accompanied by historic photographs of the funeral and tributes.

O! Temperance! was developed at The Court Theatre Training School, and originally used a cast of seventeen, as well as musicians. The irony of its title, taken from *Antony and Cleopatra*, emphasizes that its basic appeal lies in the disparity between the ideals of the characters and the norms of the audience, an incongruity which remains largely theatrical rather than social in its resonance. However, in his next work Thompson focused on issues that retain a contemporary insistence: "Songs to Uncle Scrim" was given its first performance by Downstage Theatre in 1976, and was taken on two national tours that year, gaining immediate popularity for its musical treatment of the Depression. Colin Scrimgeour, the title figure, was a Methodist minister celebrated for his radio work during the period, but he serves simply to give the show a focal referent. Depression character types are individualized briefly, they sing their songs back to their radio uncle, and they then dissolve back into their collective context which also accommodates a good deal of New Zealand social feeling of the 1970s. As in *O! Temperance!*, the group solidarity of the characters welds the audience tightly into a sympathetic but discrete unit, its theater-going impulses harnessed by the paradox of the play's genre: a musical about a depression.

"Songs to Uncle Scrim" is almost entirely sung, and for the musical score—as with *O! Temperance!*—Thompson was largely assisted by Stephen McCurdy. In "A Night at the Races" (1977), his first major work after going to Auckland, Yvonne Edwards contributed to the scriptwriting and Andrew Glover composed most of the music.

In "A Night at the Races" the theater becomes a racecourse; the program is a racebook, containing free tickets which the audience uses to place bets at totalizater booths in the auditorium. The three acts of the play follow the three "legs" of a race meeting, with videotape supplying the actual races, and, at the end, the cast applauds the "winners" in the audience, who receive free drinks or tickets to another show. Between the races, a context of ebbing hysteria heightens the drama of various characters who have come to the meeting for stock motives: to escape from marital constrictions, to pick up a girl, to strike a big win. The straightforward nature of their reasons for social convergence gives substance to their choric singing, and their paeans to the racetrack dominate the atmosphere of the theater; even the loser has the compensation of being part of the chorus and advancing the celebration. Some parts of the script, such as the interviewing team preparing a documentary on gambling, emerged as awkward accretions to the original script, blurring the impact of the surrealistic elements, in which the sinister magnetism of the horses becomes most clear; a revised version, however, has been found much more cohesive.

"A Night at the Races" develops many of the skills noticeable in Thompson's earlier work, especially in terms of audience manipulation. But its primary importance to New Zealand drama lies in its determined avoidance of elitist subject matter: the sport of betting on horses occupies a remarkable proportion of the New Zealand population, and had been a popular subject for the nineteenth-century drama of Marschel, Darrell, and others. In exploiting it on stage for the first time this century Thompson continued in his expansion of the referential basis of New Zealand drama to accommodate all prominent facets of national life, including those which people customarily go to theaters to escape.

II *Paul Maunder and the Amamus Theatre Group*

Collective theaters, developing their own scripts in rehearsal and performing in informal situations, began to appear in New Zealand in 1970. Lack of organizational stability and a generally nonliterary approach to theater meant that the impact of most of these groups was deliberately ephemeral. Some, such as Auckland's Living Theatre, were crude in their methods and eclectic in their repertoire, occasionally using conventional scripts: Living Theatre included Philip McHale's "The Island of Mulabeeka" in an otherwise group-developed program. Several young poets worked with group theaters; most notable, toward the end of the decade, was Alan Brunton's association with the satirical cabaret programs of the Red Mole company.

Two groups, however, had a sophisticated theoretical grounding which stimulated revaluation of methods within established theaters. Francis Batten's Theatre Action was formed in 1971 and consisted mainly of former students of the École Lecoq in Paris; after two years, the group was reduced in scale, but had a continued educational importance through its mask and performance workshops as well as occasional public programs. Theatre Action's most substantial specific contribution to New Zealand drama was "The Best of All Possible Worlds" (1973), a search for national identity which included Cook's discovery of the country, pioneer confrontation with the land, and the consolidation of the welfare state.

The Amamus Theatre Group, by contrast, generated its own theater methodology; although contact with Grotowski (and a study tour to Poland in 1975) was accompanied by a refinement of theatrical strategy, the group retained its original integrity. Initially, the Amamus company consisted of about ten actors and chose not to use a theater of its own, rehearsing a script for several months after it reached its final form and then presenting it in a variety of locations. However, Unity Theatre provided a sympathetic base for major public performances, and Amamus productions revitalized the Theatre's reputation for social incisiveness.

Paul Maunder, the founder-director of the Amamus group, generally occupied an editorial position over the emergent scripts. Of the earliest works, the most notable were the Depression documentary "The Wall Street Banks in London Have Closed" (1971), an exploration of a typical New Zealand upbringing *I Rode My Horse down the Road* (1971), and a documentary study of the country's major waterfront strike "Fifty-one" (1972). The published script of *I Rode My Horse down the Road* is characteristic: each of the seventeen scenes is prefaced with a statement of "situation" and "intentions," so that the motivation of each role (which is in most cases dissolved at the end of the scene) is completely explicit. The simplistic nature of each sketch, making a single point about childhood or adolescent conditioning, is accentuated by the incongruity between the actor and his role: no attempt is made to disguise the fact that the actor is an adult, and two framing scenes near the start and at the end present the parents viewing their son whom they speak of as a child but who is in bed with his secretary. The dominant theme thus becomes that of the stolid insensitivity of a society crippling itself by its inability to accommodate change.

Subsequent works deny the consolation or the logic of a frame. "Memories of Christmas" (1972), "Strangers" (1973), and "Pictures" (1973) show a development from referential specificity in the dramatized perspective toward a self-generating immediacy of expression. Between 1970 and 1973 Maunder had scripted three major works for television, and his stage works of this period mostly implied a lens as intermediary; Francis Batten had described "The Best of All Possible Worlds" as a show in which "shadows, figures and dreams of past, present and future . . . pulse and weave together as we gently split open the collective skull,"[2] and the rationale—but not the style—of several Amamus works had been similar. With "Pictures," a work on Vietnamese issues, the Amamus method shifted from the scrutiny of the regional mythology of the collective skull to the creation in the theater of mythopoetic energies without any sense of final form. This development matured with the production in 1977 of "Song of a Kiwi," a tripartite work which had been in rehearsal since 1975, and which had been presented to audiences at several intermediate stages.

"Song of a Kiwi" consists of "Gallipoli" ("an image of the past"), "Valita" ("an image of the present"), and "Oedipus" ("an image of the future"). Gallipoli was the site of a disastrous landing by Australasian troops on the Turkish peninsula during World War I, an event still commemorated by a national holiday. However, this "image of the past" is dramatically located in the present through the distribution of roles on stage, so that there is one "Kiwi" and five "Turks." The mad Kiwi soldier is shot by the Turks who, to come to terms with the invader, resurrect him and take the roles of his mother, father, wife, and mate (comrade); a priest presides over the ritual. In this way the narrative of the Kiwi's life is developed simultaneously with the advancement of the Gallipoli campaign, and the crude virility cult of the Kiwi's home conditioning blends continuously with Turkish warfare. Neither narrative is subsumed by the other; the richness of the Turks' cultural background heightens the Kiwi's impoverishment, but the Kiwi's rejection of them allows the possibility of Kiwi myth.

In "Valita" and "Oedipus" the collocation of images becomes more violent. "Valita" consists of the convergence of Kiwi, Pole, Nazi, Jew, and Mother, a sifting of cultural fragments derived from obvious sources like Sylvia Plath, Ted Hughes, T.S. Eliot, Janet Frame, and Peter Weiss, and a final reaffirmation of separate identities, with design motifs giving a dominant context of death and sacrifice. "Oedipus" echoes Hughes, Seneca, and Sophocles, but also introduces Maori verbal and performance motifs. Like "Gallipoli," "Oedipus" is performed inside a large tent-like structure inside the theater, with the audience seated around the walls; in "Gallipoli" this admits a realistic interpretation, suggesting military life under canvas, but in "Oedipus" a single central light source projects the elemental myth drama in colossal shadows on the walls behind the audience, so that the audience becomes part of the projected image of the future.[3]

To audiences who are not concerned with theory, Amamus methods are remarkable for their use of verbal crudities such as calling a Kiwi a Kiwi and using broad regional accents, the antithesis of conventional theatrical enunciation. In their aggressive use of diction and vocal color, Amamus productions achieve a tense atmosphere of national self-confrontation.

III *Craig Harrison*

The most popular exploitation of racial stereotypes in New Zealand drama in the 1970s was in the plays of Craig Harrison, a Yorkshireman who in 1966 took up a university position in New Zealand. Harrison's is a populist drama, its themes are stated heavily, its satirical targets are relatively easy ones, its comic sources are mostly familiar ones; one of his plays formed the basis for a very popular television situational comedy series. But because of Harrison's characteristic frontal exposure of his material his plays have been a valuable irritant to the New Zealand theater, their frequently cumbersome structure containing an aggressive development of theme.

Tomorrow Will Be a Lovely Day (1974) received its first performance to mark the twenty-fifth anniversary of The Elmwood Players, Christchurch, a society with a speciality for promoting local scripts; the professional premiere was delayed until Mervyn Thompson reshaped the play at the Mercury Theatre in 1978, by which time the script had found wide acceptance as a school text. The play is a political and social hypothesis which is based very firmly on a controversial reality: two Maoris walk into the National Library armed with machine guns and steal the Treaty of Waitangi, a historic docu-

ment of much-debated legality on which the British acquisition of
Maori land was principally based. Between the play's amateur and
professional premieres, the issue of Maori land had escalated to the
level of a major national problem, and Thompson's production, in a
year of police action against protest movements, inevitably had an
atmosphere of immediacy.

In the early scenes two Maoris assemble their sten guns while a
fatuous Narrator lectures the audience on Maori life, the parliamen-
tary cabinet meets to discuss the theft of the Treaty, and the two
Maoris, Matenga and Tahu, argue about their actions with a third; the
authority of the Narrator, dubious from the start, is overtly challenged by Matenga, who addresses the audience to explain his family's background, particularly Tahu's experiences in borstal, in jail, and
with the army in Vietnam. After a flashback set in Dunedin, in which
a patronizingly permissive white couple reacts against Matenga's
friendship with their daughter, a television newsreader announces
that the Maori extremists have occupied a Gisborne radio station,
that a Maori and a hostage have been killed, and that emergency
regulations have imposed curfews. The cabinet meets to discuss
military control, and an American representative offers aid; at this
stage, the American has the clearest understanding of the deficien-
cies of the local administration. Tahu consults a Maori elder arrog-
antly, and then severs his connection with Matenga; these relatively
subdued scenes come close to realism, but the atmosphere is
punctured with the appearance of a dummy prime minister who falls
apart on stage and thus allows the military to intervene, as the
American adviser had predicted. In the final scenes a soldier lectures
the audience on do-it-yourself torture techniques, the Dunedin
couple talk about Matenga being wanted, the cabinet is overrun by
the military, Tahu speaks to the audience before he is shot, and the
army interrogation expert attaches his torture equipment to the
Narrator.

Harrison's primary target, announced in the title, is the blind
optimism of the average New Zealander, typified in the legend of the
egalitarian welfare state completely without a race problem. From
realistic premises, consisting of two atypical Maoris triggering off a
latent division, Harrison cogently projects the total dissolution of the
country's democracy. The conception of the action is not, as has been
claimed,[4] unconvincing: the hypothesis is parallelled in Baxter's "The
Starlight in Your Eyes" (1967) and in C.K. Stead's novel *Smith's
Dream* (1970), and partially substantiated by military and police
action against Maori protesters in 1978. The flaws of the play lie rather

in its deployment of defamiliarization devices in a way that sometimes seems arbitrary, so that the effect is of stylistic crudeness; the verbal texture in places is allowed to develop a sustained realism that makes its puncturing seem gratuitous, the function of the Narrator is awkwardly indeterminate, and some of the comic effects are insubstantial. None of these weaknesses was conspicuous when *Tomorrow Will Be a Lovely Day* opened in 1974 because the facile optimism epitomized in the title was then a widespread social reality, but recent New Zealand history has produced defamiliarization effects that are inevitably more compelling than the play's.

Tomorrow Will Be a Lovely Day was derived from a novel that Harrison had written after his arrival in New Zealand. A subplot from the same novel provided the basis of another of Harrison's plays, *The Whites of Their Eyes*, which premiered at Unity Theatre in 1974. The same hypothetical context governs the action, with the extremists' action culminating in the collapse of government with internal intrigue, military rule, and overseas interested parties showing concern. Minor flaws in the theatrical effects, such as a very contrived attempt at a strong curtain to the first act and some incongruous expressionistic vignettes, do not significantly weaken the play's impact as a contemporary melodrama, and the central character, a Machiavellian Maori businessman, is one of Harrison's most powerful creations.

Ground Level (1974) originated from another of Harrison's novels and produced his most popular comic situation, the interaction between the Yorkshireman Joe Chapman and the Maori Koro Rauhihi, who, having just won a substantial lottery, is travelling abroad. The comic dimensions of this incongruity were extended into another full-length play, "Home Truths" (1975), and into the "Joe and Koro" television series. "Perfect Strangers" (1976) develops, but does not finally transcend, the formula of racial comedy, in the context of a Wellington student apartment; "Western Powers" (1977) has a sombre undercurrent in its comic presentation of a group of New Zealanders travelling abroad to find themselves in a context of political unrest.

The imprecisions of Harrison's dramatic writing are emphasized by the frequency of critical dissension about productions, with the author sometimes intervening to insist on his purposes. His dramatic territory is between caricature and simple realism; his plays frequently pivot on socially recognizable issues, so that straightforward situational comedies may in production assume some of the properties of problem plays.

IV   *John Banas, Dean Parker, Jennifer Compton, Frank Edwards*

Numerous provocative younger playwrights appeared in the 1970s, encouraged by a rapid expansion of production opportunities and the script development assistance of the Playmarket organization and the New Zealand Playwrights' Association. Much of their work shows tentative experimentation, but technical assurance was almost immediately apparent in some of them. Gary Langford's vein of bizarre comedy is best known from "I Love You Sylvia Plath" (1976), presenting the poetess in a mental hospital, and Michael Heath approaches the same themes in a similar mood in "Pieties" (1978), and several earlier one-act plays. Michael Wilson's "Huffers," given its first performance by the Bodgie Theatre Mob at Unity Theatre in 1978, is, like his earlier work, a revue-like search for social identity. At another extreme Michael Morrissey's "Exorcisms" (1979) consists of three succinct abstract pieces, technically as economical as Anthony Taylor's radio plays; it ran simultaneously at Auckland's professional Theatre Corporate with Simon O'Connor's "The Song of Johnny Muscle," a musical drama about a young social outsider, which had its premiere at Unity Theatre in 1976. The flexibility of Theatre Corporate was also evidenced in its mounting of Chris Shiel's "East Street" in 1978, a complex historical drama about a suspected Auckland murder in 1882. Contemporary realism is little favored by the younger playwrights, and Marcus Campbell's "The World of Good" (1977) is a notable exception, presenting a dying recluse in an arid Canterbury township. The most acclaimed of the emergent playwrights is Simon Carr, whose "The Every Weather Girl," a comedy about television, opened at Wellington's Circa Theatre in 1978, and whose "There is No God in Palmerston North" (1979) is a finely constructed radio play on the theme of childhood nostalgia. However, by the end of the decade four new writers had produced substantial bodies of work: John Banas, Dean Parker, Jennifer Compton, and Frank Edwards.

John Banas's background as a playwright was in acting and revue writing; he has performed in much of his own work and retained a revue-like facetiousness in his approach to dramatic structure. His first work to attract wide attention was a radio play, "Worth Listening To" (1973), a clumsy attempt to translate a practical joke into auditory terms. As a Downstage Theatre company member in 1974, Banas scripted and directed two extremely ambitious works, with an obvious purpose of exploring the potential of the new, intimate Hannah Playhouse which in 1973 had been constructed specifically for Downstage's needs. In "W.A.S.T.E." (Wait and See the End), Banas used a wide variety of alienation devices, including film and closed-circuit television, literally to stage an ecological crisis; the actors' script presents a drama of the rise of a dictatorship, while the other media (such as deliberately blurred camera work) cover tangential implications. Banas "set out to alienate people in terms of style so that they might take a clearer view in terms of content," and acknowledged that he "failed to find the correct balance between intellectual and emotional appeal,"[5] but his achievement is considerable when compared with Harrison's *Tomorrow Will Be a Lovely Day*, a play of the same year, with stylistic and narrative similarities. "Valdramar" (1974) is a gothic rock opera written by Banas, with assistance from Clive Cockburn and Val Murphy, both of whom had worked with him on an earlier show, "Jenifer." "Valdramar" has a deliberately naive narrative structure, but some areas of verbal and musical distinction; however, like "W.A.S.T.E." it is a work of sufficient eccentricity to have defied revival.

Banas's reputation as a revue writer was well established when in 1976 he wrote a third exercise in grotesquerie on a fascist theme, "The Robbie Horror Show"; the title parodies that of "The Rocky Horror Show," by the New Zealand writer Richard O'Brien, and alludes to the Prime Minister of New Zealand, Robert Muldoon, whom Banas impersonated in production. "Package Deal," which premiered at Circa Theatre in 1977, was Banas's first conventional full-length stage play, a detective farce with a great deal of incidental satire; much of the play has a characteristic theatrical brilliance, although the first act contains passages of low farcical intensity. "Manuscript" (1978) is a one-act play about two men reading a one-act play about themselves; the cleverness of its ending is defeated by the formulaic nature of the situation, suggesting that Banas as yet lacks the structural skills to contain his obvious intelligence and wit.

Dean Parker quickly earned a high reputation as a writer of whimsical or iconoclastic comedy with a group of radio plays in 1974. "Joe Stalin Knew My Father" shows considerable naturalistic skills in its portraiture of young people, "Never a Dull Moment, Always a Droll Tale" shifts the focus to the workers, "Where Have You Gone, Wilson Whineray, Lake Taupo Turns its Lonely Eye to You" is a wry survey of a New Zealand rise to adulthood, and "The Last Three Days" satirizes journalism through a story of two bank robbers caught in a vault with their hostages. Within a year Parker had considerably revitalized radio drama, but at about this time he turned to the stage.

Dean Parker's best-known stage play, "Smack" (1974), begins and ends with a young man, Quinn, and his girlfriend in the cab of a Bedford utility truck driving along the highway (toward the audience). Quinn is noisy, buoyant, and uncouth; the girl is subdued. As they reach Napier, it becomes clear that they are not just drifters; they have a purpose, which seems to account for the girl's reticence, and the anarchic tone of Quinn's conversation seems to become explicit when they stop outside a bank, Quinn telling the girl to drive away if anything goes wrong. Inside the bank Quinn tries to blackmail the manager into backing a drug business, using information about the manager's dead son; the manager is stubborn and, in a stylized fight sequence, Quinn apparently kills him with a knife. Back in the truck, Quinn, the girl, and a hitchhiker drive south, singing Chuck Berry's "Johnnie B. Goode" as the play ends.

Welcoming the play as "a major breakthrough in New Zealand drama," Bruce Mason wrote: "Not since the first night of Richard Campion's dazzling production of James K. Baxter's *The Wide Open Cage* in 1959 have I felt so powerfully the presence of an authentic theatrical fury and passion . . . . Mr. Parker has the best ear for New Zealand dialogue I have come across. He allows his chief character, Quinn, vast monologues of raging obscenity and eloquence, some bitter and tormented, some hilarious. There is a wild poetry in much of it and he writes marvellously rhythmical speeches. The effect is enveloping, gripping and stunning."[6]

Parker has challenged the New Zealand theater "to mount plays primarily designed to demoralise the middle class and split the intelligensia,"[7] and "Smack" shows how it may be done; the parallel between drug pushing and capitalism is latent through much of the play, but the most disorientating facet is the play's technique, the stark efficiency with which Parker fuses his simplistic story-line together with a vigorous, aggressive realism in the dialogue. Dean Parker's potential audience seems very similar in nature to Sam Shepard's, but the character of New Zealand's professional theaters makes the main-bill production of such scripts a rarity. An expurgated version of "Smack" was produced on radio in 1975, at about the same time as the Downstage Theatre late-night premiere of "Two Fingers from Frank Zappa." Parker then visited Britain and returned disillusioned by the resistance of New Zealand stage and radio to plays that are "dialectic and astonishing": "the people you want to get into your theatres start work at half-past seven in the morning."[8]

Jennifer Compton is a New Zealand actress, poet, and playwright who has done a substantial amount of her writing in Australia while retaining a close connection with the New Zealand stage. *Crossfire,* her major play, was produced in Australia in 1975 and subsequently at

Downstage Theatre under the title of "No Man's Land." The play requires a single domestic set, on which are located two actions, one in 1910 and the other in 1975. Five characters belong in 1975 and four in 1910; three pairs of characters are doubled in performance, and the use of similar names emphasizes the contrapuntal tension between the narratives. In each case the woman of the house has a pregnant maid (an "unmarried mother" in 1975), whom she attempts to use as an instrument in her feminist preoccupations; however, the doubled roles do not correlate precisely with the most obvious pairing of characters, so that, instead of the didacticism that could emerge from simple ironies, the play presents a complex network of relationships, all of which are brought into question. The structural compactness of *Crossfire*, in which figures from both periods are frequently on stage together, is lacking in "Profiles and Case Histories" and *They're Playing Our Song*, performed as a double bill in Wellington in 1976; both of these works consist of a series of sketches, mainly about simple relationships, but without any holistic coherence. Compton has written numerous radio plays, mostly for Australian production, but "An Evening with Adolf Hitler" (1977) is theatrically atmospheric in its one-act presentation of the Führer in decline, his status asserted and questioned by two unspeaking characters.

Frank Edwards is notable for his full-length stage plays belonging to a genre that is monopolized by radio and television: the success of scripts like Ian Mune's "Wild Boy Williams" (1973) on radio and Keith Aberdein's "The Governor" television drama series in 1977 makes the stage often seem a constricting arena for the historical saga or action drama. In "Bully" (1976) Edwards exploited a ready-made theatrical subject. Captain Bully Hayes was a nineteenth-century adventurer whose career included virtual piracy around the New Zealand coast and in the Pacific and theatrical promotion on the Otago goldfields, where he competed against the Buckingham family, pioneers of the Auckland stage. Edwards viewed Hayes as "the New Zealand equivalent of the Eighteenth Century Macheath,"[9] and developed the Buckinghams' theatricality to create other parallels with Brecht's *The Threepenny Opera*; however, the core of the play is its skillful realistic dramatization of a central episode in the Bully Hayes story.

"Pigland Prophet" (1978) is based on the life of Lionel Terry who, for well-publicized racist reasons, shot a Chinese immigrant in Wellington in 1905 and, after being certified insane, lived in asylums and prisons until his death in 1952. In this play Edwards complicated the chronological development by beginning with Truby King, the asylum superintendant, formally introducing Terry as a psychiatric subject; from 1916 the action advances to 1940, with Terry being deprived of all his privileges, and then goes back to 1904 for a series of scenes leading up to the murder at the end of the first act. The second act, "The Punishment," presents scenes of questioning and brutality and Terry's military memories of Africa; the last act, "The Death," is dominated by a grotesque racist parable, a dramatization of one of Terry's obscene fictions written in the asylum. "Pigland Prophet" is much stronger conceptually than in its dramatic realization; Terry's obsessions become dynamic in places, but for much of the first act many of the images seem gratuitous, aligned neither to Terry's mental state nor the audience perspective. Similarly, the notion of "Pigland" as the context that defines the prophecy is far from cogent, sometimes fiercely articulated by Terry himself, sometimes illustrated by his asylum context, and incidentally applied to Truby King, founder of the Plunket Society, "that hallowed institution that measured the future in terms of baby fat."[10] "Pigland Prophet" suffers from too many underdeveloped lines of tangential interest, any one of which might have been allowed to govern the play.

V   *Gordon Dryland*

In 1968 Bruce Mason wrote that "the quickest route for a play originating in Auckland, say, to be produced in Dunedin, is via London or New York,"[11] and the situation improved only slightly in the 1970s, so that remarkably few successful Wellington premieres result in revivals in Auckland or Christchurch. Of numerous inventive one-act playwrights in Christchurch, the best known is Eve Hughes, whose satirical comedies "The House that Jack Bought" (1972) and *Mr. Bones and Mr. Jones* (1971) have been produced in a wide variety of theaters. In Auckland two prolific writers, Alan Trussell-Cullen and Alan Williamson, have each produced technically resourceful work without as yet achieving an unquestionable major success, though both have come close; Trussell-Cullen's "Cowboy and Indians" in particular shows a remarkable refinement of comic technique. However, the one Auckland playwright of the 1970s whose work has, in quantity, penetrated every city as far as Dunedin is Gordon Dryland.

Gordon Dryland was already known as a novelist when his first major play, "Dark Going Down," was produced at Unity Theatre in 1968. The play opens with a characteristic element of moral inversion as Mark arrives home and announces to his mistress that he has been arrested again for stealing some books. Mark is aggressive, bisexual, and impolite, a combination of qualities which soon alienates the other characters; his abrasiveness governs all of them, and a conspiracy results in his pleading guilty to a variety of charges in court. Though the central action is a study of depressingly fragile relationships, considerable wit and energy are channelled through the main role.

If I Bought Her the Wool was first performed at Central Theatre in 1971, the same year as a radio adaptation of "Dark Going Down." Again, bisexuality is a central factor: William and Mabel's marriage collapsed with the birth of their hydrocephalic child, and they are now living in homosexual relationships on separate floors of an old house belonging to William's parents. The appeal of the play is largely verbal; the two men in whose apartment the play is set work in advertising and television newscasting, which gives credibility to their conversational slickness, and the situational adjustments of the five characters are drawn with considerable subtlety.

A series of radio plays, all subsequently adapted for the stage, included *Anyway—Sweet Christmas* (1972), a light family comedy, "Roman Conquest" (1974), a comedy about a couple in Italy, and "The Last of My Solid Gold Fountain Pens" (1973), a more serious study of a highly articulate couple confessing and renouncing various promiscuities. Also, in 1973, Dryland wrote a television play, "Report on Henry Bascombe," a fictional documentary about the release of a child rapist and murderer after a long jail sentence; among numerous weaknesses, this play demonstrated Dryland's dependence on quick-thinking, garrulous characters.

Two full-length stage plays were performed in 1976. "Think of Africa" presents a rich old cynic living with her sixty-year-old, hideously birthmarked son in an isolated coastal mansion north of Auckland; they are visited by the other children, fortune-hunting twins whose childhood nastiness has been projected into middle age, and the relatively intense plot makes this theatrically the richest of Dryland's plays. "Fat Little Indians" was written, according to Colin Duckworth,[12] to correct a writing mannerism: dependence on ageing characters. Accordingly, the play involves two young homosexual men and two pregnant girls combining in a sometimes witty but more often stereotyped adjustment drama. In "Aspic," which premiered on radio in 1978, a celebrity's widow undermines the prospect of a biography through the exposure of the circumstances of various relatives, including a brain-damaged son. "Casa Mabel" (1978) has another matriarch at its center, but less sophisticated than her antecedents: Mabel is among the most humanized of Dryland's characters, and serves as a focus to the intrigues of the younger people in her boardinghouse.

Though he has considerable theatrical experience and sometimes directs his own plays, Dryland's most obvious strength is verbal; one might suspect that for him the main advantage in writing for the stage lies in its greater permissiveness of expression. The limitations of Dryland's character range are clear, but within that range he is a writer of considerable individuality, with the potential of fulfilling Dean Parker's challenge "to demoralise the middle class and split the intelligensia."[13]

CHAPTER 10

The Plays of Joseph Musaphia and Roger Hall

W HILE local playwrights have supplied increasingly large quantities of scripts to meet specialized audience tastes, for the bulk of its popular productions the New Zealand theater has until recently depended on imported scripts by authors such as Alan Ayckbourn and Neil Simon. In the 1970s, however, two New Zealand playwrights have achieved a public prominence which, in Australasia, competes with that of imported comedies, so that a new work by either of them is viewed as a marketable commercial property; this is an important development because it brings the potential for self-sufficiency to the New Zealand theater, allowing more experimental writers to define their purposes more sharply.

Both Joseph Musaphia and Roger Hall were born in England and have spent most of their working lives in New Zealand, doing a wide variety of literary and dramatic work before the successes of their major comedies gave them the opportunity to specialize.

I The Early Radio Plays of Joseph Musaphia

Musaphia was educated in Christchurch and worked as a laborer, motor mechanic, commercial artist, and cartoonist until in the early 1960s he attempted to earn his living by writing for radio. When his first play was published in 1963, his optimism seemed justified, but his writing career has been fragmented by work as an actor, journalist, and proprietor of a fish-and-chip shop.

Musaphia first came to public attention with a stage play, *Free*, which premiered in the Theatre Workshop of the New Zealand Theatre Company in November 1961; it formed a double bill with Baxter's "Three Women and the Sea," and was the more favorably received of the two. *Free* involves three young men: a mechanic, a bus driver, and a house painter. It is set in the living room of their flat, and it simply reveals their apprehensions about the forthcoming

137

marriage of Phil, the mechanic, which will obviously break up their
pattern of stereotyped bachelor activities. Roger Savage analyzed the
play's serious level: "*Free* is a dialogue on liberty, on the seductive
appeal but ultimate pointlessness of cheerful drifting irresponsibility,
and the rival appeal of a stability and bolstered self-esteem which can
only be had by surrendering one's liberty to someone else . . . . The
plot is so constructed that the conflict is never resolved or judgement
finally given for either side, though by the end the prospect is pretty
dark for both. As a play of sheer argument without decisive action,
Free outstays its very real welcome . . . . "[1] The "dialogue on liberty"
certainly gives *Free* its continuity, but such a stereotyped situation is
scarcely a justification for the play as a whole. Musaphia's major
achievement was not in the dramatic presentation of serious themes
but in the play's comic elements, where his considerable talent for
caricature and naturalistic dialogue was readily employed. As a
naturalistic play about workers, *Free* was something quite new to
New Zealand drama, and it is a tribute to the enterprise of the New
Zealand Broadcasting Service that a radio version followed almost
immediately.

By the time *Free* was broadcast, Musaphia had written at least
three more radio plays, which firmly established him as a comic
writer with a special talent for masculine dialogue. "A Seat in the
Sun" has obvious affinities with *Free* in its presentation of three
factory workers watching girls during their lunch hour and in its use
of pub-style male role-playing. The conveniently existentialist tone
with which it ends recurs in "This Business of Being Alive," a domestic comedy about a young married couple and the wife's mother. All of
Musaphia's work to this point had used techniques that essentially
belong to the stage; all three plays have a single location and contain
nothing that would make them overexplicit if a visual dimension were
added. But in "That'll Be the Day" he began to explore the radio
medium, with numerous cross fades among locations—such as the
cab of a truck—that cannot readily be accommodated on the stage.
The play also shows a more assertive approach to dramatic structure,
with the action much more firmly defined than in his earlier work,
and an acceptance of the comic yarn as an end in itself. The story
simply involves some young men's attempts to force a new policeman
to ignore their after-hours drinking; it ends with an ironic twist so
that, in spite of the abortive plot, everyone is satisfied.

Musaphia's dramatic career becomes obscured, partly by pseu-
donymous writing, until 1965, when he produced two radio farces;
the second of these, "A Fair Go for Charlie Wellman," reworks the

"Yankee in King Arthur's Court" motif with a New Zealand drainlayer as the protagonist, and exploits the fluidity of radio for purposes of incongruous juxtaposition.

In "The Spook" (1966) Musaphia extended his range of characterization considerably, focusing on a middle-aged man's attempts to break away from his mother, but the context of watersiders urging him into a more adventurous social life is familiar Musaphia territory. "Be Good if You Could but You Can't" (1967) is a farce about two post office mail sorters attempting to break into an architect's safe to get privileged information on a city redevelopment plan. "Once Upon a Blind Date" (1967) again follows the love-life of some mechanics, though largely from the female perspective. In the same year Musaphia began a series of plays on Christmas themes, the best of which is the comedy "The Old Man and the Sea and Christmas Dinner" (1973).

Musaphia's radio plays of the 1960s show little development or refinement of technique, and many were obviously governed by the requirements of popular radio. From the start, his most substantial skill had been in the naturalistic presentation of working-class subjects, and he had learned how to accommodate such material within a tight dramatic structure. Most of his attempts at diversification had been unsuccessful, and he indulged his flair for caricature in two television series, "Joe's World" and "In View of the Circumstances," which he both wrote and performed in.

II *The Stage Plays of Joseph Musaphia*

In 1971 Musaphia returned to stage writing with *The Guerrilla* which, after a very successful stage premiere in Australia, was adapted for New Zealand radio. The central character, Adam King, is a familiar Musaphia type, a bus cleaner who has had a "gutsfull" of bureaucracy; with a rifle and some grenades, he assembles a heterogeneous collection of hostages in his house and spends several days waiting for a conversation with the prime minister. The situation is intensely theatrical, particularly through the play's exploitation of territorial pressures, and the central characters have considerable complexity. However, as several critics have observed,[2] the ending is very weak, with Adam meekly agreeing that he is a sick man.

The factual origin of *The Guerrilla* partly accounts for this structural weakness. Musaphia based the play on a siege near Sydney in 1968,[3] a sequence of events which, in very general terms, is represented in the play: after eight days of much-publicized manipulations of the authorities, the original urban guerrilla surrendered largely through exhaustion and demoralization. On stage, in a play that is not explicitly a documentary, one expects such an anticlimax to be corrected; Musaphia ignores many incidents—and even central characters—in the historical siege, and there is no reason why the ending should not have been shaped more strongly. But another reason for the structurally ineffectual ending lies in the central characters. At the start, they seem half-witted caricatures; Adam's girlfriend, for example, tells him that the grenades he is throwing will wake the baby. Soon, however, the naturalistic portraiture begins to command sympathy, and this emerges intermittently, particularly through the perversely cogent bond that holds Adam and his girl together on the extremity of society. It seems to be primarily this sympathy that defies dramatic resolution, but, with the relationship shattered, there is no way in which it may be articulated.

Victims (1973) is a brilliantly constructed period farce involving the most deliberately superficial of caricatures. At a graveside in about 1900 it is revealed that the deceased has left his entire fortune to Miss Madeline Gray, hitherto unknown as his bastard daughter but celebrated as the president of the Society for the Preservation of Community Standards. Once the shock subsides, Geoffrey, his publisher brother, decides to emulate his unsuspected hedonism, and dies smiling, at the final curtain, in the arms of a prostitute. Other relatives attempt to compensate for their penury by making various approaches to Miss Gray, who is independently investigating the publishing house as the source of pornographic posters. A situation thus arises admitting multiple blackmail opportunities, but only one approaches success; Sandra, Geoffrey's niece, infiltrates Miss Gray's society disguised as a man, woos and marries her, and then reveals that she expects the society to finance her life of promiscuity abroad. With the dead man's two daughters honeymooning together, the farce would seem to be consummated, but other reversals remain: notably, that Miss Gray is attracted to a life of homosexual incest.

The other characters in Victims provide elaborations on the theme of fin de siècle sexuality, their relationships intricately patterned between Miss Gray's ambivalent magnetism and that of Fabian Hathaway, pornographer, procurer, and general family leech. By distancing his material to the late Victorian era, Musaphia was able to crystallize his caricatures and thus obviate sympathy, but he also opened up a dimension of broad satire. As described within the play, Miss Gray's society blatantly parallels a similar organization in present-day New Zealand, so that the play's farcical sexual maneuvers are easily interpreted as the historicizing of Victorian puritanical repression which is still vestigial in New Zealand society. Arguing that *Victims* was Musaphia's best play to date, Bruce Mason summarized his technique as "the slyest counterpoint."[4]

Musaphia's later full-length plays alternate between farcical or satirical comedy and heavier treatments of domestic tensions. *Victims* was followed by *Obstacles* in 1974, a study of the mutual dependence and impoverishment of a weak-willed retired widower and his crippled, exploitative, middle-aged daughter who sublimates by reading erotic comics; echoes of the situation in "The Spook" become stronger when their house is invaded by Pug, a beer-swilling former boxer who drinks with the father at the pub. Misled by the daughter's *True Confessions* fantasies, Pug attempts to climb into bed with her; he is stabbed, and then blackmailed into a domestic bondage similar to the father's. The play's title refers to the imminent demolition of the house, the pub, and the associated life-styles, so that a new motorway may be constructed, and the action culminates in the collapse of the tense domestic triangle as the sound of the bulldozers comes closer. In production, the bizarre, sadistic undertones have seemed imperfectly related to Musaphia's more characteristic comic study of the beerily jocular ex-boxer, a role created by the playwright. Musaphia has argued that "the constant problem of the comedy writer [is] getting people to take comedy seriously,"[5] but he remedies the problem so thoroughly in *Obstacles* that he erects another: as in *The Guerrilla,* the problem is how seriously to take the seriousness.

Mothers and Fathers premiered at the Fortune Theatre, Dunedin, in 1975, and was quickly established as Musaphia's most popular play. It presents a domestic situation similar to that of *Obstacles,* but initially defused of sombre implications. In this play the living room is comfortably bourgeois, occupied by a lawyer and his wife whose only problem is childlessness. A newspaper advertisement for a woman to bear the lawyer's baby brings on the familiar Musaphia protagonist, this time uniformed as a traffic cop, bent on supplementing his income by exploiting his wife's breeding potential. With a discreet use of farcical contrivances, the play soon presents the traffic cop and the lawyer's wife drinking themselves into numbness and amorous compensation while the other couple consummates its legal requirements offstage. Two pregnancies eventuate, the husbands become redundant, and the comedy's serious edge becomes more insistent in

the resolution. Bruce Mason has compared the role of the lawyer with
Shaw's James Mavor Morell and Ibsen's Hjalmar Ekdal, but the part
is only Musaphia's *meneur de jeu;* the comic coherence pivots on the
epitome of antipodean citizenship, the traffic cop, another role performed by Musaphia himself, and analyzed in his preface to the
script. Of that performance Bruce Mason wrote: "Mr. Musaphia as
actor is master of the slow burn, of the slow-to-rile-but-by-God-
when-I'm-roused-I'm-ropable syndrome in town, equipped also with
a touching sense of his own dignity."[6] The gradual assertion of dignity
by the least articulate character is a pattern in several of Musaphia's
plays, and it is here fundamental to the final cohesion of the
atmosphere.

The success of *Victims* at Downstage Theatre seems likely to have
influenced Robert Lord into the mode of historicized farce with "Well
Hung," and Musaphia appears to have extended the theme with "The
Hangman" (1978). As in *Victims,* the basic technique involves the
historicizing of contemporary issues into a context of period farce;
here, the setting is in the South Island township of Picton in 1880,
where a shortage of manpower to carry out a legal hanging is disrupt-
ing the local political hierarchy. The contemporary relevance of the
play lies not in the issue of the death penalty as much as in the
pressures of parochialism, which Musaphia magnifies to ludicrous
proportions with effective use of satire. Sex farce arises from the
exploits of Picton's new policeman, viewed by the citizenry as a
matter of greater moral urgency than the imminent hanging, but
none of the nine characters has the armory of regional mannerisms on
which Musaphia's best comedy pivots, and the casuistry of the condemned man is awkward: "if a self-confessed, convicted murderer
doesn't get what the law says he deserves, New Zealand will talk of
Sodom and Gomorrah and *Picton!*"[7]

"Hunting," which premiered under Musaphia's direction at Circa
Theatre in 1979, is a major development in style and theme: a study of
the predatory basis of relationships which retains comic vigor without
attenuating the serious implications. Male stereotypes are introduced critically, not indulged for their own sake: Karl, a middle-aged,
divorced artist, has invited Todd, his boorish, wisecracking son, to
stay in his mistress Ngaire's apartment on the eve of his major
exhibition. Like Pug in *Obstacles,* Todd finds that his flippancies
make little impact on the young woman of the household; Ngaire's
daughter, Ann, embittered after an abortion and getting no sympathy
from her mother, is viciously antagonistic toward the male presence,
and her sadistic self assertion brings the play to its brilliantly succinct

resolution. But most remarkable in view of Musaphia's dramatic propensities is the reduction of the masculine clowning to the status of a function of the female dilemma, embodied in the complex, understandable—though often unpleasant—characterization of Ngaire.

In "Hunting" may be seen the fulfillment of an attempt at a more sophisticated dramaturgy dating back to *Obstacles:* Musaphia's men lose their revue-like dependence on Kiwi stereotype to become insecure loners hiding behind the facade of Kiwi stereotype, his women develop from exploitative grotesques through the caricature of Women's Rights to a huntress like Ngaire, rationally rejecting her daughter, losing her job in journalism to a younger woman, yet clinging to a precarious trial marriage as expediency makes her selective about her needs. In Ngaire, the guerrilla finds articulation and vindication.

III   *The Plays of Roger Hall*

Although it was only with the success of *Glide Time* in 1976 that Roger Hall established himself as a stage playwright, in the previous fifteen years he had written a considerable quantity of revue scripts, numerous children's plays, and several television comedies, as well as series episodes. Hall's revue work developed into a major preoccupation at teachers' training college, where he scripted for and acted in "The Rubbishers," a group specializing in political satire, largely inspired by Conrad Bollinger. In the late 1960s Hall contributed to "Knickers," Downstage Theatre's late-night revue which evolved into "Knackers," "Kniggers," and similar shows which also presented satirists like John Banas and John Clarke.[8]

From "Knickers," Hall joined Musaphia in television's "In View of the Circumstances," and wrote a number of episodes for the "Pukemanu" and "Buck House" series. In 1973 "Clean-Up," his first television comedy, was screened, followed in 1974 by "The Bach," "The Reward," and "Some People Have All the Luck." As a dramatic production medium, New Zealand television in 1973 was at a much more primitive stage of development than the radio drama department for which Musaphia had begun writing a decade earlier, and production conditions clearly limited Hall's scripts.[9] However, his television plays suggest an author acutely sensitive to his audience's receptivity, and several of the techniques basic to his stage comedies were developed here; the running catchphrases and performance mannerisms of "Buck House" are perfected in *Glide Time*, and the revue technique of paring down plot to accentuate ironies is evident in "Clean-Up" and, more extensively, in *Middle-Age Spread.*

Glide Time, which premiered at Circa Theatre in 1976 under Anthony Taylor's direction, is set in the stores department of a branch of the Public Service. "Glide time" is official jargon for flexible working hours, and the principle becomes a satiric target at the start of the first act with the discovery that Jim, the dourly self-defensive Kiwi stereotype, has slept in the office. An antipathy is established early between Jim and Hugh, a Welsh immigrant also in his forties, and the play's central filament of suspense lies in their rivalry for promotion. The seriousness of their motives gives a sympathetic edge to the last two acts, but earlier in the play their sparring is kept mainly on the level of broad satire by the intermediacy of John, a young extroverted bachelor, Michael, the ingenuous office boy, and Beryl, the stolidly mundane office spinster. The Boss and Wally, the clipboard tyrant, are purely of mechanical significance, but their deployment is sufficiently complex for this to pass unnoticed in production.

Since almost all the characters acknowledge the absurdities of the bureaucracy to which they belong, the satire is largely self-generating. Hugh has developed an aversion to the country of his unsuccessful adoption, and frequently voices his complaints. John has a strong tendency toward theatricality, which often takes the form of satire or parody of his fellow workers or social environment. Sometimes the whole office collectively makes a ritualized response to a familiar irritant. The effect of such episodes is to make it clear that much of the satire is essentially an "in joke," attributed primarily to the character rather than to the author, and this is compounded by the fact that the play is located in—and premiered in—Wellington, the center of New Zealand's Public Service. It has been seen as ironical that the play's success has been largely with audiences composed of public servants,[10] but the irony is of Hall's deliberate creation: since most of the characters are self-aware, the play is both a satire on the Public Service and a comedy about the public servant's need to see his life as satirical. The key to survival in the Public Service—or in Wellington—is laughter, but the laughter changes in quality in productions in other cities.

The resolution of *Glide Time* is achieved when, in the fourth act, all the characters converge in the office for the Boss's farewell drinks; on the telephone, Jim challenges the Director to join them, and everyone panics out of the office when the Director agrees to come. There remain, however, the problems of Hugh and Jim, both of whom have been confronted with predicaments of considerable complexity. Jim has been partially civilized by his son's rebellion, and his anarchy in the office is unconvincingly defused at the end; Hugh has been deserted by his wife when his promotion application failed, and knows he cannot integrate into either New Zealand or Wales. In humanizing these two characters to a depth well beyond satirical caricature, Hall gave the play a social resonance which has been much praised, but which is not wholly compatible with its orthodox, well-made structure.

Middle-Age Spread, which premiered at Circa Theatre in 1977, involves three couples at a dinner party on the final evening of a school term. Colin, the host, has just been promoted to headmaster; Judy, a guest, is on his staff; and Reg, his neighbor, is a teachers' college lecturer. It is on these three that the action pivots; their spouses contribute to the comic continuity by offering platitudes to cushion their severities. The story element is simple: Colin has recently concluded the only infidelity of his life, with Judy, and at the end of the play Reg, an accomplished philanderer, announces this to the whole party. The action is parallelled in the—non-appearing—younger generation, when it is revealed that Colin's daughter is pregnant to Reg's son. In *Glide Time* everyone is defeated by the laziest member of the staff whose only contribution to the action is a telephone call from his hospital bed; in *Middle-Age Spread* the parental drama is upstaged by the pregnant girl crying in her room.

Although the play's serious elements mostly emerge through the situational drama, its popular appeal has been as a satirical comedy, and this is based on character rather than situation. The spouses all approach stereotypes; Colin's wife is the hostess whose mind has stagnated since marriage, Reg's wife frantically buries herself in cottage industries to distract herself from her husband's affairs, and Judy's husband is an unimaginative, reactionary accountant. The mainly negative qualities of these characters mean that Colin and Judy become attractive by default, and their romance appears as the inevitable convergence of two people starved of intelligent and humane company. However, in Reg lies the catalyst of most of the comedy, a perverse, articulate, aggressively liberal social anarchist whose nastiness is dramatically counterweighted by the amount of convincing social comment that he offers. In the drama of emotions Reg is the heavy, the social antagonist who accomplishes verbally what his son consummates physically.

When Reg is in command of the dinner party devastation, the comedy rarely falters, but the four scenes at the dinner party are punctuated by six flashback scenes which trace the development of Colin's affair with Judy in the manner of retrospective exposition. Since Colin is a quiet, reflective character and is on stage almost continuously through the flashback scenes, it is possible to interpret them as located within his memory and hence governed by his impulse toward self-justification. However, for this subjectivity to become explicit would need blatant associative linking strategically placed near the end of scenes; but elements like the borrowing of a book that might serve to trigger Colin's memory are merely incidental, so that the retrospective scenes have an atmosphere of objectivity which exposes the crudity of the play's causation. The scenes of Colin's developing intimacy with Judy, for example, are all preceded by scenes of rejection by his menopausal wife, an implicit allocation of culpability which is so facile as to undermine any basis in serious realism.

If the comic texture of *Middle-Age Spread* largely conceals the hollowness of the play's realism, the quality of the comedy is sometimes strained by the random deployment of satire. In *Glide Time* the satire is mostly directional, consistently aimed at long-established popular targets; once it is clear which way the laughter is flowing, it continues unimpeded apart from a few deflections toward the end. In *Middle-Age Spread* the discreet charms of the New Zealand bourgeoisie are similarly self-parodying, but a large quantity of its incidental satirical allusion is simply gratuitous. When the pregnancy is discovered, an abortion is suggested, and Reg volunteers to "Do our bit to keep Air New Zealand's profit up."[11] His allusion is to the fact that New Zealand's conservative abortion legislation forces many women to go to Australia for an abortion. If taken realistically, the flippancy reveals an extreme insensitivity which subverts any remaining dimension of human values; the girl's pregnancy is no sooner discussed than it is trivialized into a basis for satire or—more generally—a debating issue. But even as an issue, unrelated to a specific pregnancy, abortion is contentious enough to split any audience, so that when Hall's random satire touches it the inevitable effect is to decimate audience laughter. In the film of the play, scripted by Keith Aberdein and directed by John Reid in 1979, these weaknesses are partially corrected by fragmenting the action into many more scenes and emphasizing Colin's perspective.

State of the Play, which premiered under Anthony Taylor's direction at Downstage Theatre in 1978, attempts to develop fragmentation as a theme. Dingwall, a once-successful playwright, is conducting a weekend course in dramaturgy in a country school; only five people have come, but they are sufficiently diverse caricatures to admit considerable interaction. Dingwall lectures on playwriting, and they combine in reducing *Pygmalion* to its essence. Dingwall then introduces a more substantial topic, their relationships with their fathers, and they create various role-playing situations, participating in each other's autobiographical sketches. When they recreate their fathers' behavior at their own births, the action is intensifying toward self-discovery; the caricatures of the first scene have been demasked, the social poses are lost to reveal raw emotions.

Although *State of the Play* was, like its predecessors, a major commercial success in its first season, critical response was, for the first time, extremely mixed; only one critic has attempted to vindicate the play in analytical detail.[12] The basic problem is that, however Hall develops it, the initial situation has the appearance of a self-conscious theatrical cliché, and this in itself alienates the interest. However intense the discrete episodes may be, the role-playing conveniently confuses therapy and art, with suggestions of Gestalt dreamwork seminars, and these are not brought back into a focus at the end. The play thus explores several layers of illusion without a yardstick of reality, and Hall's use of autobiographical material derived from his own father[13] intensifies the impression that the play is a personal statement about dramaturgy.

In 1978 Hall also wrote "Cinderella," a pantomime with a good deal of local reference which was produced almost immediately in three New Zealand cities. Like his two previous plays, "Cinderella" was completed during his tenure of the Robert Burns Fellowship for New Zealand writers at the University of Otago, and it again raised the question of the propriety of a university patronizing such conventional writing.

With the possible exception of "Cinderella," none of Hall's plays may be regarded as a mere amplification of an imported formula. *Glide Time*, structurally his finest play, builds up its own comic momentum by subjecting its characters to the most widely felt determining force in the country: the New Zealand Government. *Middle-Age Spread* is hilarious comedy to those who do not have to worry about below-average incomes, domestic comfort, abortions, or job security, people whose major concern is middle-age obesity: the New Zealand theater audience. The basis of Hall's success, apart from an exceptional skill at comic dialogue, is in intelligent research of the local market.

That Hall's research findings are sound is beyond dispute, and it is also appropriate that such research should be sponsored by a university. It is, however, not defensible that because Hall follows Merton Hodge in revitalizing well-made dramaturgy he also should be promptly compared with Chekhov, as well as Molière and Sheridan.[14] Hall himself is as unpretentious in his claims as he is in his techniques; he acknowledges his debt to—and respect for—Mason, Musaphia, and others, and high among his aims is satisfying as wide an audience as possible.[15]

Hall is not writing literary or theatrical classics, and his satire is necessarily ephemeral; the near collapse of the Public Service Investment Society in 1979 made the published text of *Glide Time* a period piece.

IV *The New Theater Audience*

New Zealand drama is a literature that has emerged in a period when, throughout the world, theater conventions have undergone frequent revolutions. Inevitably, audiences have been shattered and reorganized, and theater writing has both reflected and initiated the changing functions of drama in civic life.

The first New Zealand plays were written soon after the dissolution of the patent theater system in Britain, and New Zealand drama reached its first maturity in the late Victorian period, when the theater was a relatively egalitarian entertainment form, accessible to all and enjoyed by most. That this social function of theater was quickly usurped by the cinema is evident from the space allocations of newspapers and popular magazines, and between the wars New Zealand drama became increasingly elitist, concerned to gratify a connoisseur audience. Dramatic writing subsequently became more specialized, with poetic drama attracting closest critical scrutiny on the stage and expressionistic "dream plays" being most readily accommodated on radio. By the 1960s the stage was also feeling the competititon of the emergent television industry, and the most substantial playwrights of that decade developed their skills by radio writing and subsequently translated these techniques into the terms of the new, generally intimate, community theaters. By this development, the elitist New Zealand drama appeared to be becoming even more a minority taste.

The flourishing of both New Zealand theater and dramatic literature in the 1970s is the result of numerous influences, sociological as well as artistic, but the effect has been to make local drama a modest but undeniable source of national pride. When *Middle-Age Spread* eventually opened in London in 1979, the event received front-page newspaper attention, and when Hall's latest play, *Prisoners of Mother England*, opened in Wellington soon after, the public response was immediate and enormous. Of this last play Ian Fraser observed that the theme—migration—had been more adroitly handled by Bruce Mason in "Birds in the Wilderness" more than twenty years earlier,[16] and that Hall's use of revue techniques was taking him back to his early style, with a risk of superficiality. This is certainly true, though very few of the new audiences can be aware of it; the recent growth of New Zealand drama is dependent on Hall for economic rather than artistic reasons, and it seems inevitable that such a writer should front the movement.

While *Prisoners of Mother England* was in its premiere season, Robert Lord's "High as a Kite" opened at Downstage Theatre, Joseph Musaphia's "Hello Goodbye" and John Banas's "All Washed Up" were presented by Radio New Zealand, Gordon Dryland's "Unlikely Places" ran at New Independent Theatre, Paul Maunder's film *Sons for the Return Home* began a national screening, Mervyn Thompson established a new professional summer theater in Auckland, and The Court Theatre announced that a new play by Bruce Mason would premiere in the new year. As a new popular audience is consolidating, these more substantial playwrights, who at the start of the decade looked like pioneering individualists, are responding to the new momentum.

The importance of "the Roger Hall phenomenon" lies in defining, for the first time this century, a New Zealand mainstream theater, unashamedly middle-class and cautiously intelligent. Only now that that area has been defined may New Zealand drama await its next chapter, in which the interrupted demoralization of the middle class and splitting of the intelligensia may be continued.

Notes and References

Chapter One

1. *New Zealand Spectator*, July 8, 1848, p. 1.
2. Margaret Williams's excellent edition of *The Sunny South* (Sydney, 1975) contains a bibliography.
3. Joe Graham, *An Old Stock-Actor's Memories* (London, 1930), p. 42f. The "Middle Island" is now called the "South Island."
4. Ibid., p. 43.
5. *Otago Witness*, September 2, 1865, August 10, 1867.
6. Ibid., October 13, 1883, p. 23.
7. William Archer, *The Theatrical 'World' of 1896* (London, 1897), pp. 26–29, 277.
8. Uncatalogued playbill, Hocken Library, Dunedin.
9. *Otago Witness*, January 29, 1881, p. 20.
10. *New Zealand Sporting and Dramatic Review*, June 3, 1897, 9.
11. Maurice R. Keesing, *Dramas and Poems* (Auckland, 1909), p. 12.
12. "Uncatalogued Set 12, Item 12," Mitchell Library, Sydney.
13. Ibid.
14. Ibid.
15. Quoted in *Otago Witness*, November 27, 1880, p. 20.
16. *New Zealand Sporting and Dramatic Review*, June 16, 1904, 18.
17. Ibid.
18. *New Zealand Sporting and Dramatic Review*, March 15, 1906, 18.
19. Maurice Hurst, *Music and the Stage in New Zealand* (Auckland, 1944), p. 102.
20. Pat Lawlor, *Confessions of a Journalist* (Christchurch, 1935), p. 165.

Chapter Two

1. Alan Mulgan, *Three Plays of New Zealand* (Auckland, 1920), p. 4.
2. "Merton Hodge" was the pseudonym of Horace Emmerton Hodge; his unpublished autobiographical writings are held in the Alexander Turnbull Library, Wellington.
3. *Figaro*, May 24, 1938.
4. *Evening News*, June 13, 1932.
5. *Birmingham Mail*, February 23, 1934. The opinion is substantiated by Hodge's adaptation for English production of Sidney Kingsley's *Men in White*.

6. The principles of "well-made" dramaturgy are analyzed in John Russell Taylor's *The Rise and Fall of the Well-made Play* (London, 1967).

7. Interview with the author, 1974; subsequent quotations from Bradwell are also from this source.

8. Eric Bradwell, "Clay," in *"Clay" and Other New Zealand Plays* (Wellington, 1936), p. 11.

9. Ibid., p. 47.

10. Ibid., p. 12.

11. Ibid., p. 47.

12. Unpublished script in Bradwell's possession, p. 1.

13. J.A.S. Coppard, "Sordid Story," in *Twelve One-Acts from the International One-Act Play Theatre*, ed. Elizabeth Everard (London, 1939), p. 297f.

14. Ibid., p. 296.

15. Coppard, "Machine Song," in Everard, p. 271.

Chapter Three

1. Bruce Mason and John Pocock, *Theatre in Danger* (Hamilton, 1957), pp. 5, 36–38.

2. Peter Buck, *Anthropology and Religion* (New Haven, 1939), pp. 75–78.

3. A.W. Stockwell, "The Axe," *Landfall* 2 (1948):136–140.

4. M.K. Joseph, "The Axe," *Landfall* 5 (1951):65–67.

5. James K. Baxter, *Recent Trends in New Zealand Poetry* (Christchurch, 1951), p. 14.

6. D'Arcy Cresswell, *The Forest* (Auckland, 1952), p. 12.

7. Ibid., p. 96.

8. Ian Hamilton, *Falls the Shadow* (Auckland, 1939), preface.

Chapter Four

1. Unity Theatre's production record has been analyzed by Bruce Mason in *Landfall* 9 (1955):153–159, and in *Act* 4 (1979):37–38. For Mason biography, see McNaughton, *Bruce Mason* (Wellington, 1976).

2. Mason, *New Zealand Drama* (Wellington, 1973), pp. 56–60.

3. Mason, *The Pohutukawa Tree* (Wellington, 1960), p. 92.

4. Thomas Wolfe, *The Web and the Rock* (New York, 1939), p. 263.

5. Mason, *The End of the Golden Weather* (Wellington, 1962), p. 30.

6. Mason, *Awatea*, 1st ed. (Wellington, 1969), p. 5.

7. Mason, "To Russia, with Love," typescript in author's possession, p. 163.

8. Ibid., p. 126. The source was *Look*, September 3, 1957, 25–29.

9. Ibid., p. 126.

10. Mason, "The Glass Wig," *Landfall* 1 (1947):282–294.

11. Mason, "Beginnings," *Landfall* 20 (1966):143–149.

12. Mason, "Et in Arcadia Ego," *Landfall* 9 (1955):294–300.

13. Mason, "The Conch Shell," *Landfall* 12 (1958):302–317.

Chapter Five

1. James K. Baxter, "Jack Winter's Dream," *Landfall* 10 (1956):180; see also *New Zealand Listener*, September 19, 1958, 8.

2. Richard Sharp, review in *The Village Voice*, December 13, 1962.

3. James Bertram, "The Wide Open Cage," *Landfall* 14 (1960):81–84.

J.G.A. Pocock, review of *Two Plays*, *Landfall* 14 (1960):197–201.

4. Baxter, *The Devil and Mr. Mulcahy, The Band Rotunda* (Auckland, 1971), p. viii.

5. Hal Smith, "Baxter's Theatre: A Critical Appraisal," in *James K. Baxter Festival* [theater program], (Wellington, 1973), p. 5.

6. Baxter, *The Devil and Mr. Mulcahy, The Band Rotunda*, p. 59.

7. Ibid., p. vii.

8. Baxter, "Some Possibilities for New Zealand Drama" [transcript of radio talk delivered in 1967, Hocken Library], p. 11.

9. Baxter, *The Rock Woman* (London, 1969), p. 23.

10. Baxter, "The Day that Flanagan Died," typescript in Hocken Library, p. 11.

11. 2 Cor. 5:21.

12. Baxter, "Some Possibilities for New Zealand Drama," p. 12.

13. Baxter, "Some Notes on Drama," *Act* 3 (1967), 22.

14. Quoted in *New Zealand Stage* 1 (June 1967):6.

15. Program note, Globe Theatre Baxter Festival, January 1968.

16. Philip Smithells, "Prolific Mr. Baxter," *New Zealand Listener*, November 17, 1967.

17. Baxter, *The Sore-footed Man, The Temptations of Oedipus* (Auckland, 1971), p. viii.

18. Baxter reviewed Fry's translation [London, 1955] in *New Zealand Listener*, April 27, 1956.

19. Ibid.

20. Rodney Milgate, *A Refined Look at Existence* (London, 1968).

21. Adrian Mitchell, "Fifteen Million Plastic Bags," in *Poems* (London, 1964), p. 53.

22. Baxter reviewed Sartre's adaptation [London, 1967] in *New Zealand Listener*, December 22, 1967.

23. Baxter, *The Sore-footed Man, The Temptations of Oedipus*, p. ix.

24. Ibid., pp. ix–x.

25. Frank Sargeson developed his novel *The Hangover* [London, 1967] from the same factual basis; see *Landfall* 24 (1970):146.

26. Baxter, *The Devil and Mr. Mulcahy, The Band Rotunda*, p. 26.

27. Ibid., p. x.

28. Baxter, "Some Possibilities for New Zealand Drama," p. 13.

29. A phrase used by "M.M.," a New York reviewer of *The Wide Open Cage* in 1962; the untitled clipping is in the Hocken Library.

30. Baxter, "Some Possibilities for New Zealand Drama," p. 10.

31. Ibid., p. 16. Baxter expressed this opinion frequently.

Chapter Six

1. James Bertram, Review of *The Tree*, *Landfall* 15 (1961):266–267.
2. Sarah Campion, "No Caviare to the General," *Landfall* 13 (1959):269–271.
3. Allen Curnow, *Four Plays* (Wellington, 1972), preface, p. 12.
4. Baxter, "Some Possibilities for New Zealand Drama," p. 16.
5. MacD. P. Jackson, "Conversation with Allen Curnow," *Islands* 2 (1973):p. 158.
6. James Bertram, "Curnow Agonistes, and Others," *New Zealand Listener*, June 10, 1972.
7. Keith Sinclair, *A History of New Zealand*, revised ed., (Harmondsworth, 1969), p. 51.
8. Curnow, "A Time for Sowing," *Landfall* 15 (1961):77–79.
9. D.F. McKenzie, review of *Wrestling with the Angel*, *Landfall* 19 (1965):295.
10. An earlier version was entitled "Home."

Chapter Seven

1. Warren Dibble, "Two Stories," *Landfall* 21 (1967):89–95.
2. Dibble, "How with This Rage," *Landfall* 22 (1968):351.
3. George Webby, "The Gulbenkian Series," *Act* 10 (1970):7.
4. Dibble, *"Lord, Dismiss Us . . . "* (Christchurch, 1967), p. 2.
5. Alexander Guyan, "The Projectionist," *Landfall* 18 (1964):15–24.
6. Margaret Dalziel, "Conversations with a Golliwog," *Landfall* 16 (1962):299–300; David Hall, "Conversations with a Golliwog," *New Zealand Theatre* 128 (1962):8–10; John Dawick, "Television Drama," *Act* 22 (1974):42; C.C. Catley, "New Zealand Playhouse," *Landfall* 28 (1974):73.
7. Bradwell, "Local Drama," *New Zealand Listener*, October 17, 1969.
8. Diane Farmer, radio review, *New Zealand Listener*, April 16, 1973.
9. Webby, "The Gulbenkian Series," *Act* 10 (1970):9.
10. Baxter, review of *Maui's Farewell*, *New Zealand Listener*, September 30, 1966.
11. Copies of Campbell's drafts are in the University of Canterbury Library.
12. Farmer, "Inside the Outsider," *New Zealand Listener*, April 15, 1965.
13. Ibid.
14. Ibid.
15. McNaughton, interview with Campbell, *Landfall* 28 (1974):67.
16. Campbell, *Kapiti* (Christchurch, 1972), p. 55. An earlier version of *Sanctuary of Spirits* was published as a separate volume (Wellington, 1963).
17. Campbell, "The Suicide," *Landfall* 28 (1974):307.
18. Farmer, "Inside the Outsider."
19. These poems were first collected in *Blue Rain* (Wellington, 1967), and republished in *Kapiti*.

20. McNaughton, interview with Campbell, p. 63.

21. Baxter, *Aspects of Poetry in New Zealand* (Christchurch, 1967), p. 33.

22. Peter Bland, "From the Playwright," *New Zealand Stage* 1 (June 1967):7.

23. Jack Shallcrass, "Two New Plays," *Act* 3 (1967):5.

24. Bland, quoted in radio preview, *New Zealand Listener*, January 26, 1968.

25. Bland, "I'm Off Now," typescript in Radio New Zealand library.

26. Bradwell, radio review, *New Zealand Listener*, April 10, 1970.

27. Helen Faville, radio review, *New Zealand Listener*, June 4, 1973.

28. Peter Cape, radio review, *New Zealand Listener*, January 17, 1972.

Chapter Eight

1. Jack Shallcrass, "Original Plays at Canterbury," *New Zealand Theatre* 162 (1968):8.

2. Ronald Barker, in *New Zealand Theatre* 162 (1968):6.

3. Max Richards, "From the Playwright," *New Zealand Stage* 1 (July 1967):13.

4. Ian Fraser, "The Gulbenkian Theatre: Two Plays," *Landfall* 24 (1970):168.

5. Richards, "The Queue," *New Zealand Stage* 1 (July 1967):9.

6. Richards, "From the Playwright," 13.

7. McNaughton, ed. *Contemporary New Zealand Plays* (Wellington, 1974), pp. 110–125.

8. Interview with the author, 1973.

9. George Webby, "The Gulbenkian Series," *Act* 10 (1970):5–6; Sylvia Clayton, television review, *Daily Telegraph*, July 21, 1969; Stanley Reynolds, television review, *The Guardian*, July 21, 1969.

10. George Melly, "Picking the T.V. Winners," *The Observer*, January 12, 1969, 26.

11. Interview with the author, 1972.

12. Robert Lord, "It Isn't Cricket," *Act* 15 (1971):supplement p. 1.

13. Ibid., pp. 1–8.

14. Lord, program note, *New Zealand Listener*, August 14, 1972.

15. Arthur Allan Thomas was twice convicted of the murder of Harvey and Jeanette Crewe at Pukekawa in 1970; his conviction was still the subject of controversy when "Well Hung" was first produced, and the case was reopened in January 1975. A pardon in 1979 led to a further protracted enquiry.

16. Mason, "The Playwright, the Play and the Police," *The Dominion*, March 2, 1974.

17. Richard Campion, "Curiouser and Curiouser," *Club Newsletter* [Auckland Theatre Trust] 32 (May 1974).

18. Karen Jackman, "Lord Knows what He Wants," *New Zealand Listener*, May 12, 1979.

Chapter Nine

1. Mervyn Thompson, *First Return* (Christchurch, 1974), p. 6.
2. Program note for premiere, July 16, 1973, presented by Downstage Theatre in the Wellington Concert Chamber.
3. "Oedipus" is thus a precise theatrical realization of Plato's allegory of the cave, although there is no evidence that the parallel is deliberate. In reply to a review Maunder has commented on the evolution of the work in *Act* 2 (1977):54.
4. Philip Tremewan and Ruth Harley, review of Mercury Theatre production, *Act* 3 (1978):72.
5. John Banas interview, *Act* 23 (1974):3–4.
6. Mason, "Authentic Fury," *New Zealand Listener*, December 14, 1974.
7. Dean Parker, "Who Are Britain's Playwrights?" *Act* 1 (1976):7.
8. Ibid. See also Parker, "Factory Theatre," *Act* 20 (1973):18–20.
9. Frank Edwards, "Bully," Playmarket typescript, p. iv.
10. Edwards, "Pigland Prophet," Playmarket typescript, p. 3/6.
11. Mason, "Theatre," *The Pattern of New Zealand Culture*, ed. A.L. McLeod (Melbourne and Ithaca, 1968), p. 252.
12. Colin Duckworth, "Youthful Prototype," *New Zealand Listener*, February 19, 1977.
13. Parker, "Who Are Britain's Playwrights?"

Chapter Ten

1. Roger Savage, "One for the Price of One," *Comment* 3 (1962):10.
2. Frank Bladwell's edition (Sydney, 1976) includes criticism.
3. Ibid., pp. 55–65.
4. Mason, "Farce Revisited," *New Zealand Listener*, June 22, 1974.
5. Joseph Musaphia, *Mothers and Fathers* (Wellington, 1977), p. vii.
6. Mason, review of performance, *The Dominion*, October 30, 1975.
7. Musaphia, "The Hangman," Playmarket typescript, p. 53.
8. Roger Hall, "Memoirs of a Middle-Aged Satirist," *New Zealand Listener*, September 3, 1973, 16–17.
9. Tony Simpson, "Buck House," *Act* 23 (1974):21–22.
10. Ian Fraser, "Slide Time," *New Zealand Listener*, February 4, 1978.
11. Hall, *Middle-Age Spread* (Wellington, 1977), p. 78.
12. John Hale, "State of the Play," *Act* 4 (1979):34.
13. Hall, in "Memoirs of a Middle-Aged Satirist," attributes M. Hulot impersonations to his father.
14. Fraser, "Slide Time"; Ian A. Gordon, foreword to *Middle-Age Spread*, p. 6.
15. Anne McGovern "A Shower of Cinders," *New Zealand Listener*, December 23, 1978; see also Ann Lloyd, "The State of the Playwright," *New Zealand Listener*, August 11, 1979.
16. Ian Fraser, "Flashing through a Decade," *New Zealand Listener*, November 24, 1979.

Selected Bibliography

PRIMARY SOURCES

ADAMS, ARTHUR HENRY. *Three Plays for the Australian Stage*. Sydney: William Brooks, 1914.

ANDREWS, ISOBEL. *The Willing Horse*. London: French, 1963.

BAXTER, JAMES K. *Two Plays: Jack Winter's Dream and The Wide Open Cage*. Hastings: Capricorn Press, 1959.

———. *The Devil and Mr. Mulcahy, The Band Rotunda*. Auckland: Heinemann, 1971.

———. *The Sore-footed Man, The Temptations of Oedipus*. Auckland: Heinemann, 1971.

———. "Three Mimes." *Landfall* 29 (1975):328–333.

———. *Jack Winter's Dream*. Wellington: Price Milburn, 1979. [First published in *Landfall* 10 (1956):180–194.]

BLAND, PETER. "Father's Day." *Landfall* 21 (1967):258–292.

———. "George the Mad Ad-Man." *Act* 3 (1967):9–16.

———. "Shsh, He's Becoming a Republic." *Landfall* 24 (1970):261–279.

BOWMAN, EDWARD. "Salve Regina." In *Contemporary New Zealand Plays*, ed. McNaughton (q.v.) pp. 110–125.

———. "John." *Act* 23 (1974):15–18.

BRADWELL, ERIC. *Four One-act Plays*. London: Allen and Unwin, 1935.

———. "Clay." In *"Clay" and Other New Zealand Plays*, ed. Victor S. Lloyd. Wellington: British Drama League, 1936.

BRYANT, GEORGE, ed. *Four New Zealand One-Act Plays*. Auckland: Stockton House, 1978.

CAMPBELL, ALISTAIR. *Sanctuary of Spirits*. Wellington: Wai-te-ata Press, 1963. [Also in *Kapiti*. Christchurch: Pegasus Press, 1972.]

———. "When the Bough Breaks." *Act* 11 (1970). [Also in *Contemporary New Zealand Plays*, ed. McNaughton (q.v.), pp. 19–57.]

———. "The Suicide." *Landfall* 28 (1974):307–325.

COMPTON, JENNIFER. *Crossfire*. Sydney: Currency Methuen, 1976.

———. "They're Playing Our Song." In *Can't You Hear Me Talking to You?*, ed. Sykes (q.v.).

COPPARD, J.A.S. "The Axe and the Oak Tree," "Candy Pink." In *Five New Zealand Plays*, ed. John N. Thompson. Auckland: Collins, 1962.

———. "Machine Song," "Sordid Story." In *Twelve One-Acts from the International One-Act Play Theatre*, ed. Elizabeth Everard. London: Allen and Unwin, 1939.

CRESSWELL, W. D'ARCY. *The Forest*. Auckland: Pelorus Press, 1952.

CURNOW, ALLEN. *The Axe*. Christchurch: Caxton Press, 1949.

———. *Four Plays*. Wellington: Reed, 1972.

DIBBLE, WARREN. *"Lord, Dismiss Us . . ."* Christchurch: British Drama League, 1967.

———. "Lines to M." *Act* 10 (1970):supplement.

———. "How with this Rage." *Landfall* 22 (1968):352–363.

DRYLAND, GORDON. "If I Bought Her the Wool." *Act* 28 (1975).

———. "Anyway—Sweet Christmas." In *Four New Zealand One-Act Plays*, ed. Bryant (q.v.), pp. 9–31.

EVANS, CLAUDE. *Four Plays*. Christchurch: Pegasus Press, 1950.

———. *That Man Harlington*. Christchurch: Pegasus Press, 1952.

———. *Overtime*. Christchurch: Pegasus Press, 1955.

———. *Rich Man Poor Man*. Christchurch: Pegasus Press, 1957.

———. *So Laughs the Wind*. Christchurch: Pegasus Press, 1959.

FIRTH, JOSIAH CLIFTON [under pseudonym of Arthur Fonthill]. *Weighed in the Balance*. Auckland: Wilsons and Horton, 1882.

GUTHRIE-SMITH, W.H. *Crispus*. Edinburgh: William Blackwood, 1891.

GUYAN, ALEXANDER, [and NOONAN, MICHAEL]*Two Plays*. Dunedin: Ngaio Press, 1963. [Includes "Conversations with a Golliwog"]

———. "The Projectionist." *Landfall* 18 (1964):15–24.

HALL, ROGER. *Glide Time*. Wellington: Price Milburn, 1977.

———. *Middle-Age Spread*. Wellington: Price Milburn, 1978.

———. *State of the Play*. Wellington: Price Milburn, 1979.

HAMILTON, IAN. *Falls the Shadow*. Auckland: Griffin Press, 1939.

HAMMOND, R.T. *Under the Shadow of Dread*. Christchurch: Whitcombe and Tombs, [1908].

HARRISON, CRAIG. *Tomorrow Will Be a Lovely Day*. Wellington: Reed, 1975.

———. "Ground Level." *Act* 24 (1974):21–44.

———. "The Whites of Their Eyes." *Act* 26 (1975):23–44.

HODGE, MERTON. *The Wind and the Rain*. London: Gollancz, 1935.

———. *Grief Goes Over*. London: Gollancz, 1935.

———. *The Island*. London: Heinemann, 1937.

———. *The Story of an African Farm*. London: Heinemann, 1938. [Several of Hodge's plays appeared in Gollancz anthologies.]

HUGHES, EVE. "Mr. Bones and Mr. Jones." *Act* 13 (1971):supplement.

IZETT, JAMES. *King George the Third*. Wellington: Watts and Richards, 1899.

JONES, STELLA. *The Tree*. Christchurch: Whitcombe and Tombs, 1960.

KEESING, MAURICE. *Dramas and Poems*. Auckland: Abel Dykes, [1909].

KIDMAN, FIONA. *Search for Sister Blue*. Wellington: Reed, 1975.

LORD, ROBERT. "It Isn't Cricket." *Act* 15 (1971):supplement.

———. "Balance of Payments." In *Can't You Hear Me Talking to You?* ed. Sykes (q.v.).

———. "Meeting Place." *Act* 18 (1972):supplement.

———. "Glitter and Spit." *Act* 27 (1975):11–21.

MCNAUGHTON, HOWARD, ed. *Contemporary New Zealand Plays*. Wellington: Oxford University Press, 1974. [Revised edition 1979].

MCNEILL, BRIAN. *The Two Tigers*. Wellington: Price Milburn, 1977.
MANN, PHILLIP. "The Magic Hand." *Act* 21 (1973):23–35.
————, and JUGAND, JEAN-PHILIPPE. "Il suffit d'un baton." *L'Avant scene* 605 (March 1, 1977), 41–45.
MASON, BRUCE. *The Pohutukawa Tree*. Wellington: Price Milburn, 1960.
————. *The End of the Golden Weather*. Wellington: Price Milburn, 1962.
————. *Awatea*. Wellington: Price Milburn, 1969. [revised ed. 1979]
————. *Zero Inn*. Christchurch: New Zealand Theatre Federation, 1970.
————. "Hongi." In *Contemporary New Zealand Plays*, ed. McNaughton (q.v.) pp. 131–152.
MAUNDER, PAUL. "I Rode My Horse Down the Road." *Act* 14 (1971).
MULGAN, ALAN. *Three Plays of New Zealand*. Auckland: Whitcombe and Tombs, 1920.
MUSAPHIA, JOSEPH. "Free." *Landfall* 17 (1963):348–369.
————. *The Guerrilla*. Sydney: Currency Methuen, 1976. [Currency Double Bill, ed. Frank Bladwell.]
————. "Victims." *Act* 20 (1973):21–44.
————. "Obstacles." *Act* 25 (1974):21–42.
————. *Mothers and Fathers*. Wellington: Price Milburn, 1977.
RICHARDS, MAX B. "The Queue." *New Zealand Stage* 1 (July 1967):9–12.
————. "The Roof." *Frontiers* 1 (1968):13–20.
————. "Sadie and Neco." In *Can't You Hear Me Talking to You?*, ed. Sykes (q.v.).
————. "Cripple Play." *Landfall* 29 (1975):282–294.
ROSS, KATHLEEN. *The Trap*. London: Deane, 1952.
SARGESON, FRANK. *Wrestling with the Angel: Two Plays: A Time for Sowing and The Cradle and the Egg*. Christchurch: Caxton, 1964.
SOMERVILLE, DORA. *Maui's Farewell*. Christchurch: Nag's Head Press, 1966.
SYKES, ALRENE, ed. *Can't You Hear Me Talking to You?* St Lucia: University of Queensland Press, 1978. [Eight plays]
TAYLOR, ANTHONY. "Digby." *Act* 29 (1975):supplement.
THOMPSON, MERVYN. *O! Temperance!* Christchurch: Christchurch Theatre Trust, 1974.
————. *First Return*. Christchurch: Christchurch Theatre Trust, 1974.
WADMAN, HOWARD. *Life Sentence*. Wellington: Wingfield Press, 1949.

SECONDARY SOURCES

1. Source Guides

MCNAUGHTON, HOWARD. *New Zealand Drama: A Bibliographical Guide*. Christchurch: University of Canterbury Library, 1974. Attempts a comprehensive descriptive listing of all locatable New Zealand playscripts, published and unpublished.
NEW ZEALAND THEATRE FEDERATION. *Library Catalogue 1978*. Wellington: N.Z.T.F., 1978. A small amount of relevant material.

PLAYMARKET. *A Directory of New Zealand Plays and Playwrights*. Wellington: Playmarket, 1978. An excellent guide to contemporary material. Playmarket [P.O. Box 9767, Wellington] acts as agent for many playwrights, and in 1976 took over the publication of *Act*, changing the format and serial numbering.

2. Major Criticism and Historical Studies

BAXTER, JAMES K. *James K. Baxter as Critic*, ed. Frank McKay. Auckland: Heinemann, 1978. Contains extracts from "Some Possibilities for New Zealand Drama" (pp. 212–220).

BERRY, JOHN. *Seeing Stars: A Study of Show Folk in New Zealand*. Auckland: Seven Seas, 1964. Anecdotal personality profiles.

CARNEGIE, DAVID. "Theatre in New Zealand." *Canadian Theatre Review* 14 (1977):15–32. Accurate and succinct survey of recent production conditions.

COLE, JOHN REECE. "Merton Hodge, Playwright." *New Zealand's Heritage* 6 (1973):2387–2392. Useful biographical background, but inaccurate on the evolution of *The Wind and the Rain*.

DOWNES, PETER. *Shadows on the Stage: Theatre in New Zealand—The First 70 Years*. Dunedin: John McIndoe, 1975. A pictorial history of the period 1840–1910; interesting, informal text, poorly documented and in places inaccurate (the title of the first New Zealand play is wrong), but of some value to the student.

DOYLE, CHARLES. *James K. Baxter*. Boston: Twayne, 1976. Coverage of the plays in the context of Baxter's poetry.

EDMOND, MURRAY. "Group Theatre." *Islands* 1 (1972):157–162. The origins of Amamus, Living Theatre, and Theatre Action.

GRAHAM, JOE. *An Old Stock-Actor's Memories*. London: John Murray, 1930. Vague and anecdotal, but a unique account of the New Zealand stage in the 1870s from the point of view of a minor actor; not solely concerned with New Zealand.

HARCOURT, PETER. *A Dramatic Appearance: New Zealand Theatre 1920–1970*. Wellington: Methuen, 1978. A pictorial history very similar to Downes's, containing a great deal of valuable detail but often suspect at the level of generalization.

HURST, MAURICE. *Music and the Stage in New Zealand: A Century of Entertainment 1840–1943*. Auckland: Charles Begg, [1944]. The pioneer study of the field, a remarkable book, frustrating in its lack of source reference.

JACKSON, MACDONALD P. "Conversation with Allen Curnow." *Islands* 2 (1973):142–162. Concerned primarily with the poetry.

LAWLOR, PAT. *Confessions of a Journalist*. Christchurch: Whitcombe and Tombs, 1935. Includes "observations on some Australian and New Zealand writers," presented in such general terms that verification is often difficult.

LEEK, ROBERT-H. "Home-grown Vintage '73." *Islands* 2 (1973):315–318. On Baxter, McNeill, McNeish, and others.

McNAUGHTON, HOWARD. "Baxter as Dramatist." *Islands* 2 (1973):184–192.

———. *Bruce Mason.* Wellington: Oxford University Press, 1976.

———. (ed.) *Landfall* 29.4 (December 1975). New Zealand Drama issue.

———. "The Plays of Alistair Campbell." *Landfall* 28 (1974):55–68. Edited interview.

———. "The Plays of Bruce Mason." *Landfall* 27 (1973):102–138. Edited interview.

MASON, BRUCE. *New Zealand Drama: A Parade of Forms and a History.* Wellington: New Zealand University Press, 1973. Directed at secondary school readers; useful information on Mason's plays.

———. "New Stages in Theatre." *New Zealand's Heritage* 7 (1973):2644–2651. Recent theater history.

———. "The Plays of Claude Evans." *Landfall* 10 (1956):43–48.

———. "Theatre." In *The Pattern of New Zealand Culture,* ed. A.L. McLeod. Melbourne: Oxford University Press; Ithaca, N.Y.; Cornell University Press, 1968. General history of New Zealand theater and analysis of conditions in early 1960s, pp. 239–256.

———. "Wellington's Unity Theatre." *Landfall* 9 (1955):153–159.

———, and POCOCK, JOHN. *Theatre in Danger, A Correspondence.* Hamilton: Paul's Book Arcade, 1957. Comparison of Christchurch and Wellington theater; valuable information on Mason's early plays.

MILLAR, NOLA. "Theatre." In *An Encyclopaedia of New Zealand,* ed. A.H. McLintock. Wellington: New Zealand Government Printer, 1966. A valuable survey article, vol. 3, pp. 389–394.

———. "The Theatre in Pioneer Days." *New Zealand's Heritage* 2 (1972):796–803. Some additional information.

NICHOLLS, H.E. "Thespian Memories." *Art in New Zealand* 5 (1933):168–171, 241–248; 6 (1933), 153–159. Wellington amateur theater history since about 1870, anecdotal rather than researched, but containing a lot of accurate detail.

REES, LESLIE. *The Making of Australian Drama: A Historical and Critical Survey from the 1830s to the 1970s.* Sydney: Angus and Robertson, 1973. Particularly useful for nineteenth-century coverage; authors who worked in both countries (Leitch, Adams, Hume, Stewart, and others) are placed in context.

RHODES, H. WINSTON. *Frank Sargeson.* New York: Twayne, 1969. Sound descriptive coverage of the plays.

SIMPSON, E.C. *A Survey of the Arts in New Zealand.* Wellington: Chamber Music Society, 1961. Organizational structure.

SMITH, HAROLD W. "James K. Baxter: The Poet as Playwright." *Landfall* 22 (1968):56–62. On Baxter's 1967 stage plays.

WEBBY, GEORGE. "The Gulbenkian Series." *Act* 10 (1970):5–6. A proposed sequel article did not eventuate.

[A research program on New Zealand theater annals directed by the author is in progress at the University of Canterbury; a large amount of source material from newspapers of the period 1870–1980 is filed on computer cards.]

3. Unpublished Theses

McNAUGHTON, HOWARD. "An Examination of New Zealand Drama, with Special Emphasis on the Period since 1944." Ph.D. dissertation, University of Canterbury, N.Z., 1975.
ROMANOV, PATRICIA SINGLETON. "Towards a New Zealand National Theatre: A Study of Indigenous Professional Theatre in New Zealand 1945–1960." Ph.D. dissertation, University of Oregon, Eugene, Oregon, 1973.

Index

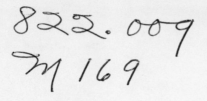